في ذكرى

مارك لينز

Falafel, hummus and doner kebabs; couscous, stuffed vine leaves and marzipan – the delicacies of the Middle East have long since found their way onto menus in the West, while spices such as cloves, cardamom, saffron and cinnamon that were once beyond most people's means are today familiar ingredients in every well-appointed kitchen. But how much do we really know about Middle Eastern cuisine?

In this book, the renowned Islamic scholar Peter Heine explains, among other things, why Muslims never eat pork, but are not infrequently partial to a glass of red wine. He goes on to describe the kinds of dishes that were prepared in the Thousand and One Saucepans of the Ummayads, Abbasids, Ottomans, Safavids and Mughals and how almsgiving came to be considered part of good etiquette at table. The author recounts tales of the great Middle Eastern chefs and cooks, both male and female, of the distribution of different vegetables and fruit across the region and the routes by which they were brought to Europe, and of how the supply of halal produce worldwide has now become a multi-million pound industry.

Since Heine is also an avid gourmet, this unique cultural history is garnished with over a hundred recipes, including everyday dishes for the modern kitchen, classic preparations from the annals of Mughal and Abbasid cookery, and lavish confections that conjure up the culinary delights of Paradise.

Peter Heine

THE CULINARY

⤜ CRESCENT ⤛

A History of
Middle Eastern Cuisine

Translated by Peter Lewis

GINGKO

First published in English in 2018 by Gingko Library
4 Molasses Row
London SW11 3UX

This first paperback edition published in 2020

First published in German as *Köstlicher Orient* by Peter Heine
© 2016 Verlag Klaus Wagenbach, Berlin

English language translation copyright © Peter Lewis 2018, 2020

Cover illustration: From a photo of an Uzbek mosaic
© Konstantin Kalishko / depositphotos

A CIP catalogue record for the book is available from the
British Library.

ISBN 978–1–909942–42–4
eISBN 978–1–909942–26–4

Layout by Denise Sterr

Typeset by Mitchell Onuorah in Minion Pro and Gill Sans

Printed in Czech Republic

www.gingko.org.uk
@gingkolibrary

Prologue

The German scholar Adam Mez, who founded the School of Islamic Studies at Basel University in Switzerland, is thought to have been the first person to produce an intensive study of the role played by eating and drinking in Islamic societies. All he had at his disposal were literary and historical sources. Accordingly, the end result was a somewhat skewed picture of medieval Oriental cuisine – by which he meant principally Arab cuisine. The first medieval Arab cookbook to come to light, which was only edited as late as 1934 by the Iraqi scholar Daoud Chelebi, was translated into English five years later by the British Arabist Arthur John Arberry. In 1949, research into the culinary history of the Islamic world took a great leap forward with the completion of a doctoral dissertation by the French orientalist Maxime Rodinson (1915–2004) entitled *Recherches sur les documents arabes rélatifs à la cuisine* ('A study of Arab documents on the subject of cookery and food'). This was the first account of Arab/Islamic cuisine to proceed from the basis of a cookbook. In addition, Rodinson, who was influenced by the contemporary 'Annales School' of French historiography, focused primarily on the social and political significance of the art of cooking in his research and addressed the question of the influence of Arab cooking on European cuisine. There followed studies of Arab cookbooks from al-Andalus (Moorish Spain) and a variety of Islamic cuisines ranging from Morocco to Indonesia, all of which have substantially enhanced our knowledge of food and drink in Muslim societies.

The great boom which has taken place in the publication of cookbooks over the last two decades or so has not passed by Eastern cuisines. Thanks to her encyclopaedic knowledge of the culinary traditions and cuisines of the Near and Middle East, the most important author in this regard has been Claudia Roden (b. 1936), who since the late 1960s has produced numerous volumes containing recipes she has collected and notes on the cultural history of food, along with anecdotes and autobiographical observations.

The majority of cookbooks on individual countries of the Islamic world are devoted to the cuisine of Morocco; the doyenne of this particular field is the French author Zette Guinaudeau-Franc. One of the first writers to introduce an English-speaking audience to the real cuisine of the Middle East was Elizabeth David (1913–1992). Her celebrated first work, *A Book of Mediterranean Food* (1950), included recipes and ingredients that harked back to the time she had spent in Cairo and Alexandria in British-occupied Egypt during the Second World War.

Further references to cookbooks and works on the cultural history of food and drink in the Islamic world can be found in the Bibliography section.

No Pork, no Alcohol

'O you who believe! – Eat of the good things which We have provided for you and be grateful to Allah if it is Him that you worship.' Thus declares Surah 2, verse 172 of the Qur'an, the holy book of Islam. Whereas other religions tend to treat eating and drinking as mere necessities for the maintenance of life, Islam also regards these functions as manifestations of the perfection of the divine creation. The Qur'an exhorts people to delight in eating and drinking. The Prophet Muhammad, who in the view of Muslim believers had the deepest, most complete knowledge of the Qur'an, called the 'uncreated word of Allah' a banquet (*ma'duba*) to which everyone was invited. For everyone who read it, the Prophet further elucidated, it offered the greatest diversity of dishes – piquant, sweet or sour. On the other hand, the Qur'an admonished the faithful not to indulge in gluttony; 'Eat and drink, but not to excess. For He [Allah] does not love the intemperate' (Surah 7:31).

Of course, in common with all other religions, Islam is not without its precepts and proscriptions. However, in comparison to the dietary requirements in Judaism, these are positively simple. In Islam, there are rules relating to eating and fasting. Prior to eating, a person must wash their hands and invoke the name of God before partaking of their first mouthful. It is equally important to eat only with one's right hand. As far as fasting is concerned, there are certain days and periods during which people are enjoined to refrain entirely from taking food and drink, others on which fasting is allowed, and finally yet others on which fasting is forbidden. Hence, fasting is prohibited on the feast days of *Eid al-Adha* ('The Feast of the Sacrifice') and on *Eid al-Fitr*, the holiday marking the end of Ramadan, the Islamic holy month of fasting, as well as on every Friday except those which fall in Ramadan. Dietary taboos, on the other hand, relate almost exclusively to the consumption of pork and alcoholic beverages. To the devout Muslim, pork in any form is *harām* – that is, strictly forbidden.

For instance, Surah 2:173 clearly states: 'He has only forbidden you what dies of its own accord, blood, the flesh of swine, and that which has been dedicated to other than Allah.'

Why no pork?

Muslim exegetes and commentators of the Qur'an, as well as Jewish scholars who have pronounced on the comparable proscription in the Old Testament (Leviticus 11:7), and finally Western cultural studies academics have put forward numerous theories as to how the ban on pork first arose. Medical arguments are frequently cited. Trichinae (parasitic roundworms) in pork can cause serious illnesses. When these pathogens were first discovered in the 19th century, Jewish, Christian and Muslim theologians alike regarded it as being proof of the wisdom and truth of their holy scriptures. However, the real reason for the proscription should rather be sought in theological thinking. In the ancient Middle East, pigs were sacrificial animals slaughtered in honour of heathen gods and goddesses. The ban on the consumption of pork was intended therefore to set Jews and Muslims clearly apart from the devotees of the deities of the ancient East and classical antiquity even where everyday practices were concerned.

Muslims have a deep aversion, even disgust, towards pork. Even if they have inwardly distanced themselves to an extreme degree from their religion, they still forego consumption of this meat. It can easily happen that a Communist of Arab descent, who is by no means averse to a glass of whisky, will criticise an Egyptian Muslim female colleague for eating ham. Likewise, the Tatars of Central Asia often have no problem with drinking alcohol, but only very rarely eat pork. In spite of the long period of anti-religious propaganda in the Soviet Union, their intense dislike of pork has remained.

Moreover, the taboo relates not only to the consumption of pork but also to the use of pigskin and pig's bristles.

In addition, Muslims avoid gelatine, even when used in the manufacture of medicines. Contemporary Muslim scholars of Sharia law disapprove of coreligionists working as waiters in restaurants where dishes containing pork are served; their advice is to only take such jobs when no other employment is available.

According to the *ahadīth*, the body of reported words and actions of the Prophet Muhammad that have been handed down and which along with the Qur'an are counted among the authoritative texts of Islam, Muslims should also refrain from eating predators or raptors. In general, they should avoid all foods that are commonly regarded as repellent. This derives from the fact that, generally speaking, everything which is seen as unpleasant also counts as unclean. A person becomes unclean through contact with unclean things. As a consequence, all of his or her spiritual observances, such as the fulfilment of religious duties, are rendered null and void and have to be repeated in a state of ritual purity.

Ritual slaughter

When the Qur'an, in the aforementioned Surah 2:173, speaks of 'what dies of its own accord' (in other translations, simply rendered as 'carrion'), it means the meat of mammals or birds that have not been ritually slaughtered. This rule therefore does not apply to fish or other aquatic animals. Special regulations exist for ritual slaughter. As far as possible, the animal must be turned to face in the direction of Mecca. Then the phrase 'In the name of God' (*bi-smillah*) must be uttered before the animal is put under the knife, a procedure that involves severing the carotid arteries and allowing the beast to bleed to death. This practice is not only employed for the acts of ritual slaughter on *Eid al-Adha*, the principal feast day of the Muslim calendar, but also at other times. In traditional Muslim societies, in which slaughtermen and butchers are entrusted with this practice, Muslims are certain of obtaining ritually clean (*halāl*) meat.

In the light of the globally expanding food-processing industry and the international distribution of its products, as early as the 1970s there ensued among Islamic legal scholars a debate over whether, for example, deep-frozen chickens from Spain or Denmark could be considered *halāl*. In proffering their expert opinion, most of the scholars referred to a statement made by the Prophet Muhammad which permitted his followers to accept invitations to dine from Jews and Christians. For in these instances, it was reasonable to assume that the animals which were brought to table had not had the name of a heathen God intoned over them when they were slaughtered. Rather, it was highly probable that the name of the God common to all three great monotheistic Abrahamic religions had been spoken. However, the scholars engaged in this debate stated unequivocally that meat from countries with communist regimes could not be consumed, since atheists would certainly not have invoked the name of God. Major international meat-processing and packing concerns now therefore ensure that they have corresponding certificates issued by the Muslim authorities in the producer countries testifying to the ritual cleanliness of their products. In so-called 'white meat' (i.e., poultry) abattoirs run by Muslim owners, even in Europe, Muslim clerics are present during the automatic poultry-slaughtering process, whose purpose is to repeatedly recite the phrase 'In the name of God'; in view of the highly automated production line, the tempo of the operation and the noise in such plants, this ritual is apt to strike the non-Muslim observer as somewhat strange.

In certain European countries such as Denmark, Iceland, Norway, Poland or Switzerland, animal welfare regulations are in place preventing the slaughter of any animals without first stunning them, even for exclusively ritual purposes. In other words, there are no legal exemptions for *halāl* or kosher meat, which therefore has to be imported. The most important producer of such meat for export is France. In the United Kingdom, ritual slaughter is permitted as such, but under strict provisions which require that animals are properly and humanely restrained, and that stunning equipment is kept close at hand for use should the animal suffer avoidable pain, agony or agitation. To ensure rapid bleeding, knives must be sharp and well maintained and both the carotid arteries and the jugular veins (in cattle, sheep and goats) or both carotid arteries (in birds) must be severed. However, fierce debates continue to rage over the cruelty of ritual slaughter without first stunning the animal, and recently there have been moves in some local authorities to ban the supply of non-stunned *halāl* meat to state-run schools. In practice, though, in the UK some 85 percent of *halāl* meat is already stunned before the animal is killed.

When Muslims find themselves obliged to eat food prepared by non-Muslims, there is often the fear, despite reassurances to the contrary, that the meat they are served has not been slaughtered in accordance with the ritual requirements of Islam. Many thus prefer to opt for a fish dish or a vegetarian meal instead. Scepticism towards meat from unfamiliar butchers can also be seen between the various denominations of Islam: in the 1980s, for instance, the regime of the Iraqi dictator Saddam Hussein invited Egyptian farmers to resettle in Iraq and offered them very attractive conditions. This was clearly a strategy to try and weaken the indigenous Shiite population who lived in the region earmarked for the settlement area and who were opposed to the rule of the Sunni-dominated Arab Socialist Ba'ath Party under Saddam. In a study conducted by an Arab sociologist, all the Egyptian farmers who participated in the scheme praised the good relations they had with their Shiite neighbours, though whether they did so out of political opportunism or conviction was a moot point. Yet in response to the question of whether they would ever buy their meat from a Shiite butcher, they replied: 'Oh no, who knows what those people do to the meat!'

The proscription against alcohol

While pork was clearly proscribed right from the very earliest days of the history of the Islamic religion, the situation with alcohol (a term which actually derives from the Arabic word *al-kohl*) is somewhat more complex. In early revelations to the Prophet, wine from vines is regarded as something positive. In Surah 16:67 of the Qur'an, therefore, we find the following: 'And from the fruits of palm trees and grapevines you derive intoxicants as well as wholesome provision. Surely there is a sign therein for those with the faculty of reason.'

At this stage, then, fruits and the alcoholic beverages derived from them were still being described as manifestations of Allah's benevolence. In Surah 4:43, a later revelation, though, there is already a distinctly admonishing tone on this matter: 'O you who believe, do not come to pray while you are intoxicated until you know what you are saying.'

And finally, in Surah 5:90, an injunction to avoid alcohol entirely is formulated: 'O you who believe! Intoxicants and games of chance, idolatrous sacrifices at altars and divination by shooting arrows are all abominations, the handiwork of Satan. Therefore eschew such things in order that you might prosper. Satan's plan is to stir up enmity and hatred between you, with intoxicants and gambling, and distract you from the recollection of Allah, and from prayer. Will you not then abstain?'

Yet at first the rejection of alcohol did not assert itself with the same strictness as the ban on eating pork. At the outset, therefore, wine was not construed as being *harām*, but instead was categorised by Muslim scholars as 'distasteful' (*makrūh*). Their judgment was complicated by the fact that wine is mentioned in the Qur'an's descriptions of Paradise. In Surah 56:18–19, there is talk of '…vessels, pitchers and a cup of wine from a flowing spring, from which they will develop no headache, nor will they be intoxicated.'

As with numerous other statements in the Qur'an, Muslim commentators have also struggled over the past fourteen centuries to arrive at a unanimous judgment on this question. Some have even sought to interpret it as a justification of wine. Their initial approach was strictly philological, in ascertaining that the Arabic word for wine in the Qur'an was *khamr*, namely 'wine from grapevines'. Yet as is well known, wine can also be produced from other fruits. For example, a wine fermented from dates was widespread. This wine was called *nabīdh* rather than *khamr*. But because the Qur'an took a critical view of *khamr*, but not of *nabīdh*, date wine was deemed permissible. And because Arabic has more than 150 separate terms for wine, the degree of latitude regarding the ethics of wine consumption is extremely broad. Medieval Arabic literature satirised this in a multitude of anecdotes; in one a pious scholar is offered a glass of *nabīdh*, which he happily drinks, followed by a wine by the name of *kumait* (a red wine), which he also downs without demur. Finally, when he has drunk enough or his hosts are loath to serve him any more, they deliberately bring out a bottle of *khamr*, which he indignantly rejects.

The scholar al-Jubba'i (d. c. 915) developed an original line of reasoning in this regard. He considered wine made from dates as permissible. His rationale for this was that God had created and allowed things in this world which were akin though inferior to those things that the Blessed were able to enjoy in Paradise. Accordingly, human beings would strive to reach Paradise by living a life that was pleasing to God here below. The same logic applied to *nabīdh*, which was deemed to have an inferior quality in comparison with *khamr*. Another line of argument did not touch upon philological aspects, rather it maintained that the Qur'an only banned intoxication and not alcoholic drinks as such. In other words, moderate consumption was always possible. In view of these numerous uncertainties, up to the 14th century Muslims of all strata of society only adhered in a limited way to the ban on alcohol. In addition, comparatively large minorities of Jews and Christians living under Muslim rule were allowed to produce and consume alcoholic beverages, and not just on ritual grounds. The Christian innkeeper and his hostelry became common motifs in the extensive body of poetry on the subject of wine drinking that developed in the Arabic, Persian and Turkish languages. And finally there were also some Muslims who did not observe the alcohol ban at all and who quite openly sought to indulge their love of wine. Thus, the poet Abu Nuwas (d. 815) writes:

Come, pour me a cup of wine,
And as you do so proclaim that it really is wine.
Don't replenish my cup surreptitiously.
When you can do it out loud.

The Persian poet, astronomer and mathematician, Omar Khayyam (d. 1131), even attacks the advocates of a ban on alcohol when he imagines himself having a fictitious dialogue with the Prophet Muhammad:

You should go to the Prophet and say:
Khayyam sends his greetings to you and asks of you:
How is it that you permit me to drink sour milk
But expect me to forego sweet wine?

The poet then has the Prophet respond to this question as follows:

Go to Khayyam and tell him:
Only a fool could ask such senseless questions.
My prohibition of wine doesn't apply to the wise man.
I just have to ban the stupid from drinking it.

The Syrian theologian Ibn Taimiya (d. 1328) took issue in a series of legal rulings (*fatwa*) with the various arguments for a more liberal attitude towards the consumption of alcohol, finally arriving at the conclusion: 'Even the smallest amount of a substance which causes drunkenness when taken in excess is to be forbidden.' Over time, this strict attitude would take an ever firmer hold on Muslim society.

The adoption of Western habits of consumption by the middle and upper echelons of Islamic society in the period from the late 19th to the mid-20th century saw a rise once more in alcohol usage, though this was now focussed primarily on high-proof European spirits such as whisky and cognac. Illicit drinking took place either in people's homes or in international bars and hotel restaurants. In addition, homemade aniseed-based spirits such as arak or raki were also drunk; when mixed with water, these took on a white, milky appearance, hence the alternative Syrian term for arak, *halīb al-asad* ('Lion's Milk').

Since re-Islamisation, which began in the late 1960s, the question of alcohol consumption has been exploited with ever-increasing dogmatism in clashes between opposing political factions. Representatives of Islamist parties accused the ruling elites of not taking Islam seriously. To corroborate their charge, they cited the fact that alcohol was freely served on state-owned airlines, or that such drinks could be bought in state-run shops. In view of this criticism and out of political expediency, therefore, many regimes began to take a more censorious attitude toward all forms of alcoholic beverage. However, as a rule, they did not introduce a blanket ban. Only in a very few states, for example Saudi Arabia and Iran, is there a general and strict prohibition of alcohol.

In other Muslim countries, it is the case that primarily visitors from the West are exempted from any such ban. One of the largest producers of red wines in the world is Algeria. These wines are exported and blended with more exalted grape varieties from the wine-growing regions of the respective importing countries. Religious scholars barely raise any objections to this practice.

Blood

Whereas Muslim scholars still wrestle with the question of dietary rules relating to pork or alcohol, their deliberations on the subject of the consumption of blood have been far less frequent. In the play *Faust* by the German writer Johann Wolfgang von Goethe, the character Mephisto maintains that 'Blood is a quite special kind of juice', and this attitude also holds good in Muslim societies. It is claimed that the consumption of blood can lead to people contracting diseases through the transmission of pathogens. Yet this explanation is a post-hoc rationalisation. In many cultures, including Islam, blood is regarded as the seat of all life. In the ritual slaughter of animals, it is not collected but is allowed to spill on the ground. While the flesh of the sacrificed animal is either eaten by the faithful or distributed to the needy, the actual offering to God in the sacrificial act is the blood. It belongs to God alone, and is therefore *harām*. This is a perfect illustration of the ambiguity of this term.

Blood is sacred, and because it is sacred it is also forbidden. (Nonetheless, the majority of Muslim scholars raise no objections to the practice of blood transfusion.) Blood is naturally out of the question as an additive to any form of foodstuffs – devout Muslims even find themselves repulsed by the sight of red meat juices. During official visits by Eastern potentates to European capitals, many a chef responsible for preparing a state banquet who has cooked fine lamb fillet rare to accord with the Western tastes has ruefully come to the realisation that the foreign guests would have found the meat more palatable if it had been served well-done.

Yet more rules

Alongside these strict nutritional taboos, there is also a whole series of other rules. These include, as already noted above, the injunction that Muslims should not eat the flesh of predators or raptors. It has been debated whether certain fish such as eel or sturgeon – and above all caviar – are allowed. The Prophet Muhammad instructed his acolytes to moderate their intake of aromatics such as onion and garlic. In particular, he demanded that they refrain from eating either of these raw before they attended the mosque. The same stricture applied to leeks. Word-for-word, his pronouncement on this matter that has been handed down to posterity runs: 'A person who eats onions, garlic or leeks should not approach the precincts of our mosque. For the angels will be just as perturbed by it as the human beings.'

Reference should finally be made to a proscription that at first sight does not remotely belong in a culinary context. The use of gold and silver is forbidden, at least where men are concerned. This applies not only to clothing textiles such as brocade, as well as to jewellery of all kinds, but also to tableware. Thus, the account of one of Muhammad's followers informs us: 'The Prophet forbade us from drinking from vessels made of gold and silver, or from eating off them, and also from putting on garments of silk and brocade and sitting down in them.' This gave rise to a special goldsmithing technique which on the one hand satisfied Muhammad's commandment while still offering people the opportunity to flaunt their economic power and their exquisite taste in public. This technique became known as damascening. It involved taking a product made of a less valuable metal and engraving a deep groove in it. A wire made of silver or gold was then hammered into this groove. Damascening effectively circumvents the Prophet's ban on precious metals and yet still draws attention not only to the prosperity of the owner of the tableware but also to their feel for elegance and their aesthetic sensibility. By contrast, the Prophet raised no objection to the use of porcelain plates, though these luxury goods were widely known on the Arabian Peninsula as a result of the growth in international trade at that time.

Preferred dishes

In addition to proscribed foodstuffs, Islamic traditions also identify a series of preferred foods. First and foremost among these is camel meat. The Prophet Muhammad is said to have opined on this subject: 'Anyone who does not eat of camels does not belong to my people.' Nowadays, camel flesh is still one of the kinds of meat traditionally eaten at Ramadan. However, the dish that the Prophet was particularly fond of was *tharīd*. He praised his favourite wife Aisha in his assertion that, 'The virtue of Aisha over other women is akin to that of *tharīd* over all other dishes.' *Tharīd* was a kind of casserole prepared on the basis of a meat stock. This stock was thickened with finely grated breadcrumbs or with flour. The meat was boiled on the bone in the stock before being removed, stripped off the bone and put back into the stew. Vegetables and spices could then be added or alternatively a paste made of dates, clarified butter and curd cheese. The Prophet did not rate other recipes of his age so highly, but still stressed that they were not *harām*, such as a dish made from lizards, curd cheese and clarified butter. A broth known as *maraq*, containing strips of dried meat and squash, was also highly prized at the time of the Prophet. This was eaten together with barley bread. There are also reports from this period of a wheat or barley porridge called *sawīq*, which was served in various consistencies. It could be so dense that one evidently had to chew it, but on other occasions so thin that one could drink it. Two more soup-like dishes were also known during the Prophet's lifetime, *hazīra* and *harīra*, both of which were very simple preparations. *Hazīra* is a broth made from water and bran. *Harīra* was a gruel with a milk base; the only component it has in common with the well-known soup from Morocco, which is eaten at the end of fasting, is its name.

In the early Islamic period, meat was only eaten on special occasions. This is still the case for many people in Islamic societies today. The most important such feast day is the slaughtering of animals that takes place at *Eid al-Adha*.

On this occasion, devout Muslims will slaughter different animals according to their financial means. For poorer people, this might be a pigeon or a chicken, whereas the well-off will sacrifice cattle or camels. Anything that a family cannot consume is distributed to the needy. Lamb and chicken are particular favourites for special feasts; in earlier times, however, donkeys and horses were also eaten on these occasions. Rabbits were especially highly prized among game animals. As regards particular cuts of meat, the shoulder and saddle of all animals were preferred. The methods of preparation were legion. The meat was fried or spit-roasted over an open fire. Alternatively, it was baked in a *tannūr*, a clay oven.

The most common seasonings were salt, which was evidently easy to preserve, and vinegar. In addition, there was a piquant sauce called *sināb*, made by grinding together mustard seeds and raisins, which was served as a condiment with meats. Honey was used as a sweetener. Once when the Angel Gabriel (in Arabic: Jibril) mentioned the sweet known as *falūdhaj* to the Prophet, it caused Muhammad to sigh audibly. Muslim exegetes offer no explanation for his reaction. Was it that he had simply been reminded of the sheer pleasure of this dish, or did his reaction result from never having tasted it before? Whatever the case, the angel's description was only very brief. All he said was that it was made from honey and clarified butter. The dish, whose name comes from the Persian, was a favourite dessert during the era of the Abbasid dynasty. Many recipes exist for *falūdhaj*. One that was devised for serving to caliphs runs as follows:

Falūdhaj for the caliphs

The following is a translation of a medieval recipe in Arabic from the *Kitab al-Tabikh* ('Book of Cooked Food') by the 13th-century writer al-Katib al-Baghdadi.

Take as much good-quality white (clover) honey as you like, and pour it into a *tanjīr* (a copper pot with a rounded base). Heating gently, bring it slowly to a simmer, skimming off any scum that forms on the surface. As soon as it comes to the boil, pour it through a filter (*rāwūq*) and then return the filtered liquid to the cleaned pot, to which you have previously added a quantity of freshly pressed sesame oil equal to half the amount of honey. Meanwhile, over a low heat warm cornstarch with cold water, rosewater and camphor in a green glazed earthenware bowl until the mixture is dissolved. The quantity of the cornstarch mixture should be one-fifth to one-sixth of that of the honey, while the added water should weigh the same as the combined liquids. When the honey and sesame oil have returned to the boil, add them to the starch mix. Keep stirring until the mixture begins to thicken and the oil separates and rises to the top. Keep agitating the mixture with a metal spatula to prevent it from sticking to the bowl. Taste the starch mix beforehand to check that it isn't too tart, and sweeten if necessary. If you want to give the pudding a yellow colour, add some saffron to the starch. If you like, you can also toast a handful of flaked almonds and stir them in. When the oil has risen, take the bowl off the heat and spread the *falūdhaj* onto a clean, hard slab that has been liberally coated with pistachio or almond oil. Dust with icing sugar that has been mixed with musk oil and serve.

The culinary promises of Paradise

In contrast to Christianity, Muslim conceptions of Paradise as the place where the blessed may dwell for all eternity are extremely hard and fast. In the Qur'an, Paradise is portrayed down to the last detail as a magnificent garden. There are descriptions of wonderful houses inhabited by the blessed, of splendid cushions for them to recline upon, and of exquisite food and drinks for them to partake of. Black-eyed virgins of Paradise and beautiful youths wait on the blessed men and women. The meat that they eat is chicken (Surah 56: 21).

Apart from that descriptions of food in Paradise are all of a rather general kind. There is talk of fruit, and specifically of bananas. Palms are mentioned, leading us to assume that dates are eaten. Beyond this, we learn of pomegranates (see the extensive description of Paradise in Surah 55: 46–78). On the other hand, there is a wider range of accounts of the drinks that are served there. In Paradise, people are allowed to drink from gold and silver vessels. Four different types of drink are to be had there, as outlined in Surah 47: 15: 'Here is the parable of Paradise which the God-fearing have been promised: it has rivers of unpolluted water, rivers of milk unchanging in taste, rivers of wine that is delicious to those who drink it, and rivers of strained honey.'

Furthermore, these drinks are perfumed with various expensive spices such as ginger, camphor and musk. Even though these descriptions have been seen by modern Islamic commentators as nothing but symbolic signifiers of the extraordinary nature of Paradise, Muslims down the ages have preferred to take them at face value, all the more so since they are corroborated by a number of the extant *ahadīth* attributed to the Prophet. These latter depictions overtrump the descriptions in the Qur'an: 'When the beloved worshipper of Allah has grazed on the fruits of Paradise and eaten his fill, he feels an urge to eat a square meal. And so Allah commands that such a spread should be laid out before him… Each dish contains 70,000 different kinds of foods; no fire has come too near to them, no chef has cooked them, nor have they been boiled in a copper vessel or anything else of the kind, but rather Allah commanded; "Let it be so!" and they transpired without the slightest effort or difficulty… Then the faithful representative of God was gripped by an urge to taste the flesh of birds, and at Allah's command, a dish of whatever kind he desired appeared on his table, ready roasted, and he devours the meat to his heart's content.' Evidently, meat was a special dish even for the blessed in Paradise, and the quantity plays a decisive role here.

In other words, there can be no question of fasting in Paradise. That is reserved for the denizens of Hell. Surah 88: 2–7 of the Qur'an states: 'On that day many faces will be downcast; having toiled in this world only to weariness, they will enter the hot burning fire to roast, they will be given water to drink from a boiling spring, no food will be there for them but a dry, thorn plant, which will neither nourish them nor do anything to assuage their hunger.' Commentators on the Qur'an have interpreted these verses thus: 'The only sustenance available in Hell comes from thorny desert scrub, whose fruits may be likened to the head of a devil. These are so dry that anyone who ingests them finds that they stick in their throat.' Drinks in Hell are no less unpalatable. The texts tell not only of scalding hot water but also of the ensuing discharges from the flesh and the skin of the sinners. As an alternative, sinners in Hell are given a warm, fluid oil to drink, which causes their skin to peel off when they bring their faces close to it.

Rules for fasting and meals for religious festivals

One of the principal duties of Muslims is to observe the commandment to fast during the holy month of Ramadan. This is formulated in several passages in the Qur'an, for example in Surah 2: 183–185: 'O you who believe that you are enjoined to fast just as those before you were so enjoined, as a way of teaching you to become God-fearing, observe this and fast for the prescribed number of days. But whoever of your number is ill or on a journey, then let them fast for the same number of days [after Ramadan]. For those who are capable of fasting but still do not do so, there is an expiation, namely feeding a needy person for each day missed… And that you fast is better for you if you know. The month of Ramadan is that in which the Qur'an was revealed, as a guidance to men and as a clear proof of that guidance and of the criterion for judging.'

And a little further on in the same chapter, it is decreed: 'On the night of the fast, you are permitted to have congress with your wives… and to eat and drink until the whiteness of the day becomes distinct from the blackness of the night at dawn' (Surah 2: 187).

Fasting in Islam thus differs markedly from the Christian practice of eating less or of foregoing certain foods like meat entirely, though this can be substituted with fish or seafood.

Because the Islamic calendar is based on the annual lunar cycle, the fasting month of Ramadan migrates throughout the entire solar year. It can therefore fall in one of the winter months, with their very short days, or in the summer, with its long days and intense heat. Nonetheless, especially in the past couple of decades, fasting has become an ever more prevalent practice among Muslims irrespective of the climatic conditions. Public life in Muslim countries is organised around the month of fasting. Shops and state institutions open later in the morning, while newspapers and the various electronic media devote a larger proportion of their content to religious themes. First and foremost, however, people's private lives are geared entirely to fasting. Ramadan is the month in which family relations, contacts with neighbours and friendships are fostered more intensively. Conflicts that have arisen over the course of the preceding year are set aside, not least through making numerous reciprocal visits. These invitations and visits occur in conjunction with the nightly ritual of breaking the fast (*iftār*). Political parties and institutions also invite people to take part in *iftār*. This celebration can be held in the street or on public squares on long communal tables that have been specially set up there, in the headquarters of the institutions in question, or in rooms in the parliament building. These official functions often provide plenty of material for discussion the following morning. Above all, people talk about the dishes that were served. Alongside the religious aspect of the occasion, social and political factors play a major role in these public form of breaking the fast. Government representatives issue invitations as a way of demonstrating their power.

The leaders of militia groups or party organisers attempt to use such occasions to rally the support of their followers for their personal ambitions or their political programmes. Conversely, the people who participate in the *iftār* events demonstrate their loyalty by attending. Neighbours exchange dishes, and in the process it is not uncommon for a playful rivalry to arise regarding the quantity or the quality of the food people have cooked.

At both public and the private *iftār* events, typical fast dishes are served. Following the example of the Prophet Muhammad, the faithful commence proceedings by eating three dates. If the season and market conditions allow, even before the *iftār*, those who are fasting prepare little dishes containing fruit salad, which they can eat immediately after the day's fasting period has ended. Particularly juicy fruits are favoured. Apart from that, there are some regionally very diverse dishes which are eaten specially on the occasion of breaking the fast. In Morocco, there is *harīra*, a soup made from legumes. There are as many recipes for *harīra* as there are Moroccan cooks.

Harīra

The following recipe derives from various field studies conducted in the 1990s. Chicken or cheap boiling cuts of beef can be substituted for the lamb.

Heat some oil in a large pan and fry 2 finely chopped onions and a 500-gram lamb shoulder, cut into bite-sized pieces, until the onions are translucent but not browned. Add a pinch of saffron threads, 1 teaspoon ground turmeric, finely chopped root ginger to taste (around 1 teaspoon) and a litre of cold water and bring to the boil. Then tip in a can of drained chickpeas and simmer gently for 30 minutes. While the soup is heating, in a blender blitz together 5 fresh tomatoes with their skins and seeds removed, a small bunch of flat-leaf parsley and leaf coriander, and add these to the lamb, onion and chickpea mix, together with 250 grams of red lentils plus a pinch of black pepper and cinnamon, and cook until the lentils are soft. As a finishing touch, boil small soup pasta shapes (e.g. orzo) in water until they are *al dente* (around 3 minutes), drain and add to the soup. Season to taste with salt and serve in deep bowls topped with three dates (preferably fresh) per person.

Harīra is also a great favourite among members of the Jewish community from Morocco who emigrated to the United States. They adopted the traditional Muslim dish for breaking the Ramadan fast as part of the meal that has recently become customary to serve after the fast day of Yom Kippur (the Jewish Day of Atonement).

Turkish Muslims break their fast by eating *Ramazan-pide*, a bread sprinkled with sesame seeds. A more substantial dish on this occasion is a tripe soup called *işkembe çorbasi*. On the day before major feast days – especially the night preceding the 27th of Ramadan, the *Laylat al-Qadr* ('Night of Destiny'), in which according to tradition the first verses of the Qur'an were revealed to the Prophet – many housewives in Turkey customarily make three different types of pastries: *lokma* stands for the seal of the Prophet, while the written edict of the Prophet is represented by *katmer* (filo pastry) and *pishi* (baked choux pastry) stands for his blessing.

Lokma

According to the account given by the eminent Turkish cultural historian and chef, Nevin Halıcı, each of these pastries were prepared at the Ottoman court using only one teaspoon of dough apiece. There are also many different versions of this popular confectionery.

On the day before making the pastries, make a syrup consisting of 250 grams of sugar, 250 millilitres water and the juice of one lemon. The next day, dissolve ½ teaspoon of dried yeast in 25 millilitres warm water with an added pinch of sugar, sift 150 grams durum wheat flour into a bowl, create a dip in the centre and pour the yeast and water mixture into it. Knead until you have a smooth, elastic dough. Cover the bowl and put aside in a warm place until the dough has risen. Then take the dough out of the bowl again and, making a dip in the centre, add 150 millilitres water and work in thoroughly. Put the dough, in the covered bowl, back into a warm place and let it prove until the dough has doubled or even tripled in size. This stage can take up to one hour. When it is ready, using a teaspoon form little balls of dough and fry them in hot oil. Place them on kitchen paper to absorb any excess oil and then immerse them in the cooled syrup for several minutes before serving.

Similar pastries are eaten in Iran to break the fasting period. In the case of the pastry called *zulbia*, however, the dough is refined by the addition of yoghurt and rosewater is added to the syrup. Rice puddings or milk-based soups are also often consumed at this time, while a saffron rice mix served as an *iftār* dish involves a considerable financial outlay. The numerous sweetmeats and confectioneries prepared by Iranian housewives, in many cases weeks before the start of the fasting month, are particularly popular post-fasting snacks.

Because the necessary ingredients are, in some cases, extremely expensive, and since prices tend to rise steeply during Ramadan due to an increased demand, many households start systematically setting aside funds to pay for these future expenditures several months in advance. Many sweet dishes have unusual names such as 'women's navels' or 'lips of beauty'. As many women in the large cities of the Islamic world now go out to work for a living while still having to do domestic chores, they will often buy the confectioneries for Ramadan ready-made from market stalls or specialist bakery shops – much to the chagrin of their traditionally minded mothers and mothers-in-law.

The nights of the month of Ramadan are characterised by a mood of celebration and joy. Carousels and other fairground rides are set up on public squares. One may be fortunate enough to still encounter a storyteller. The streets and public buildings are lit with colourful strings of lights and special Ramadan lanterns. Shortly before the beginning of each new fast day, young men parade through the streets of the villages and city districts playing drums and other musical instruments, waking up those who are still asleep so that they will have an opportunity for a hearty breakfast before the fasting begins again at daybreak. In the middle of Ramadan, children or young people who are taking part in the fasting for the very first time are presented with small gifts. Traditionally the month of fasting would end when two reliable witnesses reported to the political or religious authorities that they had seen the new moon rise. This information would then generally be rewarded with a gift of money. Nowadays the end of Ramadan in the Islamic world is announced through electronic media. The conclusion of the month of fasting is marked with a two-day festival known as *Eid al-Fitr*.

As well as Ramadan, there are also a number of other Islamic festivals in which food and drink play a role. *Eid al-Adha* ('The Feast of the Sacrifice'), which commences on the 10th day of the month of pilgrimage and is celebrated throughout the Islamic world, recalls the incident when Abraham (Ibrahim) was about to sacrifice his son Ishmael (Isma'il) at God's behest. At the last moment, Ishmael was saved through God's intervention, and a lamb was sacrificed in his place. Many millions of pilgrims travel at this time to the holy sites of Islam in Mecca and Medina in order to carry out this sacrifice as part of their pilgrimage ritual. Throughout the world, Muslim families slaughter an animal (or have it slaughtered on their behalf) – according to their income, a smaller or a larger animal, of which they only eat a part themselves, the remainder being given to the poor. In the easternmost states of the Arab world, the feast provides an opportunity to prepare a special dish that is designed to feed a large family.

Mansaf

This recipe comes from an interview with a cook in a traditional restaurant in the Jordanian capital Amman.

In a very large pan, sweat ten large onions, peeled and coarsely chopped and ten crushed garlic cloves in hot fat (ideally, the fat from a fat-tailed sheep, though vegetable oil will also do), then add 5 to 6 kilograms of braising lamb, roughly diced, and fry it until browned. Cover with water and let it simmer until the meat is tender and cooked through, occasionally skimming the surface to get rid of the scum that forms there. Remove the lamb from the pan and keep warm. Into the remaining stock, put 250 grams of yoghurt, stabilised to prevent it from flocculating. This can be achieved by beating the yogurt with a little cornmeal (i.e. fine polenta) or an egg – one tablespoon of cornmeal and one egg white for every litre of yoghurt. Now add 3 tablespoons of lemon juice to the stock/yoghurt mixture, along with salt, black pepper, and ground cardamom or cinnamon according to taste. To serve, slice large Arab flatbreads into broad strips and lay them on a large plate *(mansaf)*. Pile the lamb on top of the flatbread, and surround it with a ring of boiled white rice sprinkled with pinenuts and almonds that have been briefly toasted. Then carefully spoon the yoghurt and stock mix over the lamb; any leftover sauce can be handed round in a separate serving bowl.

On the occasion of the great ritual observances through which Shiite Muslims commemorate the martyrdom of Husayn ibn Ali, the grandson of the Prophet, on 10th Muharram, the first month of the Muslim calendar, which take the form of mourning processions and passion plays, a confectionary called *rāhat halqūm* is served. This is made from cornstarch, sugar, pistachios, raisins and nuts. The Shiite mourning procession is known as *ashūra*; deriving from this, another dish (*ashūriyya*) is served in addition to *rāhat halqūm*.

Ashūriyya

In the view of Arab Sunni Muslims, the name of this dish, which is prepared on the anniversary of the death of Husayn, the grandson of the Prophet, is connected to the stranding of Noah's Ark on the slopes of Mount Ararat after the Flood. According to this tradition, the dish contains all the ingredients that were still to hand on the Ark after the Flood subsided.

Thoroughly rinse 250 grams of coarse bulghur wheat, 125 grams of dried white beans (cannellini or haricot) and 125 grams of dried chickpeas and soak them overnight in a bowl of cold water. Then put all these ingredients together in a large pan with 2 litres of water over a high flame. Once it has come to the boil, reduce the heat and let the pulses and cracked wheat simmer until they are tender. Then add 125 grams of rice, bring the pot back to the boil and continue cooking for another 20 minutes over a low heat. To finish the dish, stir in 100 grams of toasted almonds, and a generous pinch each of salt and sugar. Keep simmering gently until all the ingredients are tender and the liquid has reduced and the dish takes on a thick, creamy consistency. Add a little hot water at the end of the cooking time to loosen up the dish slightly and stir to prevent any sticking. If desired, you can add 1 tablespoon of rosewater to the finished dish, and garnish the individual servings with a sprinkling of chopped dried figs, dried apricots, dried plums and walnuts.

From the 8th century onwards, a strain of Islamic mysticism – Sufism – developed in Mesopotamia (modern Iraq). Over the following centuries, it gained an increasing number of followers and was organised into large hierarchically structured communities that were designated as 'orders'. The orders numbered, and still continue to this day to number, millions of members. Even at the earliest stages of their history, the Sufi orders were engaged in charitable activities. They offered simple overnight accommodation to travellers and set up soup kitchens run by professional cooks to cater to the poor, primarily in the major cities.

One of the most well-known of the Sufi orders is the society of the Mevlevi, which is particularly widespread in Turkey and which was founded on the teachings of the mystic Jalal ad-Din Rumi (d. 1273). The Mevlevi founded monasteries in which their followers lived, worked and performed ritual observances. In a monastic community of this kind, the kitchen, which was regarded as a sacred place, played a central role. Among other religious duties, the disciples were required to spend 1001 days in the kitchen and perform all the tasks, however menial, that were demanded of them as helpers. In this way, their qualities of patience, obedience, humility and composure were put to the test and exercised. From the works of Rumi and the handbooks kept by the various heads of the order, scholars have been able to extensively piece together the organisational structure of the Mevlevi monasteries, along with the daily round of duties there, including the preparation of meals. Many of the everyday activities had a religious significance in the eyes of the Mevlevi. For example, Rumi wrote: 'No sooner is the pan hot than the chickpeas start jumping up in hundreds of manifestations of ecstasy.' Another time, he noted: 'Shortly before daybreak I heard a voice cry out in excitement: the wonderful aroma of *kalye* and *borāni* wafted up to me.' *Kalye* was a generic term for dishes that involved roasted meat; *borāni* is a dish of vegetables and yoghurt. The mystic was thus using the aroma of cooking to symbolise the proximity of the divine.

Spinach *borāni*

There are many versions of this recipe, with or without rice. The key factor common to all of them is the combination of spinach and yoghurt. If the rice is omitted, it takes a mere 5 minutes to prepare the spinach. Deep-frozen spinach can also be used; in this case the quantity should be reduced to 300 grams.

Wash and roughly chop 500 grams of spinach and cook for 5 minutes in the water that clings to the leaves, then drain. Melt a knob of butter in a pan and brown 1 finely chopped onion, then pour in 250 grams of boiling water or lamb stock, together with the drained spinach and 100 grams of parboiled rice; add salt to taste. Bring back to the boil before reducing the heat and simmering until the rice is done and no longer chalky.

Leave the mixture to go cold, then stir in 250 grams of thick yogurt and two crushed cloves of garlic, along with a pinch of salt and a splash of water. Drizzle the dish with melted butter or extra-virgin olive oil.

Secular festivals

Some feast days, such as the Persian and Kurdish New Year festival of *Nowruz*, are still widely celebrated in Turkey, Iran, Iraq and the Central Asian republics despite their pre-Islamic origins. Following periods in which it was banned, it has once again become an official festival at which the political elites of the countries in question are happy to make a public appearance. *Nowruz* is held at the time of the vernal equinox. On the preceding Wednesday, youths make merry in the streets of Iran with a great deal of noise and fanfare. In the villages, a carnivalesque figure does the rounds, asking for small donations. The high point of the festival is the day of the equinox. In people's homes, a table is spread with the so-called 'tablecloth of the seven S's', the *sofreh-ye haft sin*. Its name comes from the fact that it must be laid with seven items that all begin with the letter 'S' (Farsi: *sin*). Traditionally, these are: *sabzi*, the new green shoots of wheat, barley or lentils; *sepand*, the wild rue plant; *sib*, apple; *sekkeh*, coins; *sir*, garlic; *serkeh*, vinegar; and *sumagh*, the berries of the sumac bush.

However, other objects beginning with the letter *sin* can also be substituted. The various items have a symbolic significance. *Sabzi* signifies youth and fertility, *sepand* protects a person from the evil eye, and *sib* stands for love, fruitfulness and immortality. The coins denote prosperity, while the garlic and the sumac berries symbolise good health. On the last and thirteenth day of the New Year festival, families traditionally make an excursion out into the countryside. On this occasion, some people cast the green shoots from the *sofreh-ye haft sin* into flowing water. These excursions provide an opportunity for a lavish picnic.

Nowruz was also celebrated in Egypt up until the beginning of the 20th century. However, here this festival was associated with the beginning of the

Coptic year, and hence took place on 10 September. Gifts were exchanged and special dishes eaten on this occasion. Over the centuries, it became a kind of carnival, at which representatives of authority were sprayed with water or pelted with rubbish and pestered for small sums of money or other gifts. Similarly, carnivalesque practices can still be found today in the Ashura festivals held in North African countries; the only thing these celebrations have in common with the mourning processions of the same name in predominantly Shiite societies is the fact that they both occur within the first ten days of the first month of the Islamic calendar, Muharram. In these festivities, young men still parade through the villages of Morocco, asking for presents and spraying all those who refuse their request with water. The customary dish at Ashura is a kind of beef roulade, which involves seven green ingredients being wrapped in a thin slice of beef. Because the month of Muharram can fall at various different times of the solar year, these ingredients vary according to the season. However, the similarities with the practices of the *Nowruz* festival are clear. Ashura, too, may therefore ultimately derive from a former pre-Islamic rite of spring.

Religious minorities in Islamic societies

Until the mid-20th century large minority communities of different denominations of Orthodox Christians and Sephardic Jews still resided in many regions of the Middle East; Jews had been living in Iraq since the period of the Babylonian Captivity in the 6th century BC. Today the Middle East remains home to a number of smaller religious communities such as the Druze, the Alawites, the Sabaeans or the Yazidis. From a culinary point of view, there are many similarities between these groups and the Muslim majority, but also some differences.

What they all had in common was a fundamental interest in food and its preparation. Many cultural exchanges took place in this regard which transcended both confessional and ethnic divides. What differences there were arose from the respective religious dietary proscriptions.

⚜ ⚜ ⚜ ⚜ ⚜ ⚜ ⚜ ⚜ ⚜ ⚜ ⚜ ⚜ ⚜ ⚜ ⚜ ⚜ ⚜ ⚜

Skhīna

The quantities in this recipe are meant to feed 8–10 people. Preparation of this dish should be timed so as to be completed by the start of the Sabbath on Friday evening, so that the *skhīna* can then slow-cook in the oven at a low setting.

In the base of a large pot evenly spread out 500 grams chickpeas that have been soaked overnight and then drained (or simply use pre-soaked tinned chickpeas). Take 6 threads of lightly crushed saffron steeped in a teaspoon of warm water, salt, one tablespoon of vegetable oil, 1 whole clove of garlic (cleaned but not peeled) and 10 stoned dates and lay them on top of the chickpea layer. Do not stir. Then add 1 kilogram of diced stewing beef together with a piece of chopped marrowbone. Meanwhile, in a bowl, combine 500 grams of lean minced beef, 100 grams of crumbled beef fat, 3 tablespoons of fine breadcrumbs, salt, pepper, a generous bunch of finely-chopped flat-leaf parsley, 2 whole eggs, and 2 tablespoons of oil. Using clean hands, thoroughly blend these ingredients and form them into a roll measuring around 10 centimetres diameter; wrap this 'sausage' in a clean piece of muslin and place it next to the meat. On top of this, place one kilogram of peeled and washed medium-sized potatoes. A few raw eggs in their shells can also be added to the mix if desired. Cover the whole thing with cold water and bring to the boil over a medium heat, then transfer to an oven to cook overnight at the very lowest setting. Leave in the oven until midday the following day. Serve the individual elements of the *skhīna* in separate bowls.

The most well-known and culinarily interesting of these proscriptions is the Jewish precept that people should refrain from doing any work on the Sabbath. Accordingly, Jewish housewives are obliged to prepare dishes on the Friday that take until Saturday to finish cooking. One example of this is the recipe known as *dafina* or *skhīna* among Moroccan Jews, which in the interim has become a classic dish of Moroccan cuisine.

Skhīna was able to make this transition into the mainstream of Moroccan cuisine because neither its ingredients nor its method of preparation violated any of the dietary proscriptions of Sharia Law. However, there is one major culinary distinction between the communities professing the three great Abrahamic religions. This concerns the use of fat or oil. Muslims and Jews cannot, of course, use pork fat, and in addition Jews do not use butter or butterfat. Instead, they use sesame oil. Because this gives off a very distinctive smell when heating, Jewish housewives in Baghdad switched over to using largely odourless kinds of oil once these became widely available. Christians, on the other hand, cannot use butter during Lent and instead cook with olive oil during that period. Muslims prefer the fat that comes from fat-tailed sheep.

The childhood reminiscences of writers from a variety of religious backgrounds frequently refer to experiences with the foods of other faith communities. For people enjoyed swapping various recipes. Even though some of these accounts may sound like somewhat rose-tinted recollections of the good old days, there is no doubt that social cohesion among the different faith and ethnic groups was strong thanks to their shared interest in food and eating. Reading these autobiographies, one gets the impression that all things to do with food and cooking formed the neutral starting point for relations between the different groups. The wars, ethnic cleansings and other conflicts that erupted in the second half of the 20th century have now effaced all the former knowledge of shared experiences at the dining table. At present, the only attempts to uncover this past history are taking place almost exclusively among the various Middle Eastern émigré and refugee groups who are living cheek-by-jowl with one another in Europe and the Americas.

A Thousand and One Saucepans – Cooking Among the High and Mighty

Hospitality

Right up to the present day, in societies of the Near and Middle East hospitality is one of the essential traditions of social interaction. It is practised by ordinary people and the elites alike. The greatest host of all time in the Muslim culinary tradition – as recounted in numerous reports from the early history of Islam – was a young Arab by the name of Hatim al-Ta'i (d. 605). According to tradition, even when he was still a youth he invited an entire tribe of Bedouins who were passing by to come and dine with him. To cater for them, he ordered his father's hundred camels to be slaughtered to provide a grand banquet. When his father rebuked him sternly for what he had done, he defended himself by saying: 'But father, my deeds will ensure us lasting fame among all the Arab tribes.' And he was quite right; even nowadays the phrase 'He's more generous than Hatim al-Ta'i' is commonplace among Arabs as a way of acknowledging and showing one's gratitude for a host's hospitality. Moreover, the 1990 Bollywood film *Haatim Tai*, directed by Babubhai Mistry, further served to boost the reputation of the legendary host in cinemas and on the Internet.

Of course, for Muslims the true epitome of hospitality was always, and still remains, the Prophet Muhammad. Several proclamations of his concerning this virtue have been preserved for posterity. Many of these dictums impart a perfectly pragmatic message: 'A meal for one person can also stretch to two; while one for two people can stretch to four, and one meant for four people to eight.' Because no social distinctions were to be drawn when eating together, Muhammad also demanded of hosts: 'If one of your servants avoids generating too much heat and smoke when preparing your meals, you should take him by the hand and sit him down next to you. If he does not want to do so, then take a portion of the food he has made and give it to eat.'

The significance of the communal ethos at mealtimes is also expressed in another tradition: 'The Prophet owned a huge cooking vessel called *al-gharra*' (Arabic for 'The Magnificent'), which was customarily carried around by four men. When Muhammad and his followers had said their morning prayers, this enormous pot would be brought in, full of porridge, and they would all gather round it to eat. As their numbers steadily grew, the Prophet took to kneeling when eating (in order to make more room). Seeing this, a Bedouin once asked: 'What kind of sitting position is that?' The Prophet replied: 'Allah has turned me into a generous servant; He has not made an unjust despot of me.' He then continued: 'Eat from the edges of the pot and leave something over. In this way Allah will send His blessings down upon it.'

Orthodox Islam states unequivocally that the Prophet Muhammad did not perform any miracles. After all, he was 'only' a man. Nonetheless, certain traditions in Muslim folklore still contain accounts of Muhammad performing extraordinary feats in feeding people, which are strongly reminiscent of the Biblical story of the 'Multiplication of the Loaves and Fishes' as recounted in the New Testament (Gospel According to St John, chapter 6, verses 1–15). One such account, in verse form, was written by the grammarian Qutrub (d. 821):

The tharīda *is only enough for one person.*
But a multitude ate their fill of it. No one had ever seen such a thing.

Three hundred were fed and sated by it,
Though it shouldn't have been enough to feed ascetics in loincloths.

Twenty-one dates were left in the sack, it is said.
This was reported by people who are sticklers for the truth.

And yet three thousand people had their hunger stilled.
Their bowls were refilled over and over from what remained in the bag.

The dishes that Hatim al-Ta'i offered his guests would surely have been of an inferior culinary quality. On journeys across the deserts of the Arabian Peninsula, people would have had to fill their bellies with whatever was to hand, and this could occasionally be some quite extraordinary fare. As a general rule, people ate everything they could lay their hands on, provided it wasn't unsanitary or poisonous.

Lizards and locusts were counted a delicacy. When asked one time by the Umayyad caliph 'Abd al-Malik (d. 705) what his favourite dish was, a Bedouin is said to have replied: 'A young camel with a firm hump, slaughtered when it is still healthy and not yet sick, cooked in bubbling cooking pots and carved up with eager knives on a cold morning.' There is no mention here of any special spices or methods of preparation. This simplicity in preparing food was in turn attributed to the example of the Prophet Muhammad. His favourite dish was reputed to be the *tharīda* that is mentioned in the first line of Qutrub's poem. This was a plain soup made from meat or vegetable stock and with bread dipped in it. It was especially popular when spiced with black pepper.

Tharīda (modern version)

This recipe comes from the Persian Gulf region. Other names for this dish are *tashrīb* and *fatta*.

Roughly chop one large onion and sweat it in oil in a deep frying pan or casserole until soft; meanwhile, divide a chicken weighing 1 kilograms into eight pieces (two thighs, two drumsticks and two breasts, each cut into two through the cartilage of the breastbone, leaving the wing attached to the top portion of each breast). Leave the skin on and fry in the hot oil along with the onion; when all the pieces are evenly browned, pour over 250 millilitres of chicken stock (preferably fresh, though a stock-pot or cube will do). Simmer gently with a lid on the pan until the chicken is just cooked through and tender. Remove the chicken pieces and debone, discarding the skin and the bones. Chop the meat into small pieces and return to the pan. Season with finely chopped garlic, salt and pepper, adding pinches of any or all of the following dried spices to taste: ground allspice, ground cardamom or the North African spice blend *ra's al-hānout* (Arabic, literally meaning 'head of the shop', i.e. the best spices on offer). Keep simmering on a low heat for another 15 minutes. At the end of the cooking time, add three peeled, cooked and diced potatoes and a small tin of chopped plum tomatoes. Once the soup has heated through, lay pieces of dried flatbread (or toasted cubes of white bread) on the base of serving bowls. The finished chicken stew should have a consistency like that of porridge. Ladle the stew over the bread and serve piping hot.

There is also a bread-based soup similar to the traditional *tharīda* which comes from Egypt. This is eaten during the Feast of the Sacrifice, on 10th Dhu'l-Hijjah, the final month of the Islamic calendar, and is also distributed to the poor.

Bread soup

In a saucepan, make a stock consisting of 500 grams of stewing lamb (bone in, and cut into bite-sized pieces), salt, pepper, and water to cover; simmer while skimming off the scum that forms on top. When the meat is tender, strip it off the bones and return it to the stock with 250 grams of white long-grain (basmati) rice. Cook over a medium heat for a further 20 minutes. Roughly tear some stale flatbread into pieces and put it in the base of a large soup tureen. While you are waiting for the rice to soften, peel 4 cloves of garlic, squeeze through a garlic press and fry in hot olive oil until the aroma rises. Deglaze the garlic frying pan with a good splash of fruit vinegar; let the mixture bubble up and then pour over the dry bread. The bread should absorb all the mixture and become saturated. Tip the lamb broth with the meat and rice over the bread and serve.

Entertaining guests is now a firmly established feature of the Middle Eastern way of life. Even as late as the second half of the 19th century it was still the custom at several Middle Eastern courts only to enquire what a guest desired after three days. For that initial period, it was taken as read that you were obliged to offer him accommodation and food. This clear temporal limitation enabled you to ask a guest to move on after that time had elapsed without thereby sacrificing your reputation as a good host. There were of course some people who ruthlessly exploited these traditions of hospitality. Arabic literature was well acquainted with the figure of the sponger, for whom a special term was even coined: *tufailī* (literally meaning 'infantile person').

There are a host of anecdotes describing the antics of *tufailī*. The sponger tries to justify himself with such amusing and quick-witted verbal formulations that the assembled company, whom he has interrupted, cannot find it in themselves to be truly angry with him and invite him to come and eat with them. For example, in one story a *tufailī* approaches a group of people at dinner and enquires: 'What's that you're eating?' To try and put him off, the head of the house replies: 'It's poison.' Undeterred, the sponger takes a seat among the guests and announces: 'Well, if you're all about to die, I don't want to live any longer either.' These scrounger stories appear relatively early in the history of Arabic literature and were favourite tales to pass on from one generation to the next, on account of their humorous content. Nonetheless, the behaviour portrayed is not condoned, and to this day this kind of conduct reduces such people's standing in the community. It therefore comes as no surprise to discover that scroungers are customarily given derogatory names like *ta'abbata sharran*. This somewhat unwieldy insult translates literally as 'someone carrying something disgusting under their armpits.'

The Umayyads

The simple fare of the nomadic Bedouin and the settled traders of the cities on the Arabian Peninsula that was consumed before and during the Prophet Muhammad's lifetime and the period of the earliest Muslim communities all but vanished in the first fifty years after conquering Muslim armies became acquainted with the culinary riches of Mesopotamia, Iran, Syria and Egypt.

The new elites that developed in Damascus, the capital of the Umayyad dynasty (661–750), and in the major provincial capitals gave themselves over to excess in this regard. The very first of the Umayyad caliphs, Mu'awiyya (r. 661–680) was renowned as a gourmand. The Arab historian Ibn al-Tiqtaqa (d. 1309), whose works date from after the reign of the dynasty that followed the Umayyads, the Abbasids (750–1258), as a Shiite frequently spread anti-Umayyad propaganda. He wrote the following account of Mu'awiyya's daily bill of fare: 'He ate five times a day. And one of these mealtimes was a very extensive affair. On such occasions, he was wont to instruct his servant thus: "Take it away. Although I haven't yet eaten my fill of it, I'm bored."' And the writer al-Tha'alibi (d. 1038) described a later Umayyad caliph, Sulaiman Ibn 'Abd al-Malik (r. 715–717), as an out-and-out glutton, and gave a graphic account of how he ate himself to death: 'One day, he devoured thirty chickens, followed by a hundred eggs, washed down with several mugs of date wine. He then proceeded to sleep with four virgins. But this time he had overdone it. He lapsed into a coma, and he was carried off by Fate.'

There is a paucity of information on the dishes of this period. But clearly quantity took precedence over quality. Certainly, writers of the Umayyad period are full of praise for the culinary delicacies that they have tasted. Whether this was an accurate reflection of the real situation is lost in the mists of time. In any event, we learn what marvellous things the desert had to offer. Thus, the late Umayyad poet Abu l-Hindi (c. 750) ironically praises the treats to be found there:

> *I have eaten lizards and not recoiled.*
> *I love dried strips of cured mutton at any time.*
> *I smeared butter on dates to decorate them.*
> *What fine food with exquisite garnishes!*
> *I found fungus under thorn bushes that I ate with butterfat,*
> *Camel livers with fat from its hump is really nice*
> *I give heartfelt thanks for roasted lamb on a cool day.*
> *But rice pudding and large fish make me unwell.*

The Abbasids

This plain but hearty bill of fare changed under the rulers of the Abbasid dynasty; governing from Baghdad in Mesopotamia, they constructed on the banks of the River Tigris one of the most magnificent capital cities in the world at that time. Under the influence of Graeco-Roman and Iranian traditions, an advanced civilisation developed there, one manifestation of which was its cuisine. Baghdad was the centre of a complex and highly efficient trading network, which brought goods from the four corners of the known world to the bazaars of the city and from there to people's kitchens. Olive oil came from Greece and Italy, while a whole variety of spices was imported from India and Southeast Asian islands. Meanwhile, meat and oils, wheat and rice and vegetables and fruit all came from the 'immediate environs' of the city. For instance, when it was in season, asparagus from the Ghota, the market-garden oasis of Damascus, was sent by relay post to Baghdad, where it arrived within two days. However, such things were a luxury which only the court of the caliphs and other high-ranking officials such as the vizier or the chief postmaster – who at the same time was the head of the secret intelligence service – could afford. Hand in hand with exotic ingredients from foreign lands came the corresponding methods for preparing them. Yet the changes in the culinary culture were also down to the cooks, female and male, who came to Baghdad from the territories under Abbasid control either of their own volition or as slaves. So it was that the caliph Haroun al-Rashid (r. 786–809) was sent by his half-brother, Ibrahim ibn al-Mahdi, a Byzantine slave called Bid'a. The name means 'excels at all things'. Bid'a was known far and wide as a talented chef, and was especially famous for her desserts and cold dishes. The caliph al-Amin (r. 809–813), a son of Haroun al-Rashid, heard about her culinary skills and requested her to prepare him a dish of *sikbāj*, such as she had once cooked for him and his father. He told her that he had never tasted anything as good. Bid'a naturally complied with his wish. The name of this dish came from the Persian and translated roughly as 'a kind of vinegar'. What made Bid'a's preparation of this dish so special was that she began by smoking the meat in expensive incenses like ambergris and aloe. She served the *sikbāj* with various different sausages and flatbreads filled with finely chopped meat and pickled vegetables, as well as little pastries and an assortment of vegetables and herbs arranged in such a way that they resembled a flower bed. The caliph was ecstatic and on the spot composed a poem beginning with the lines:

> Here comes Bid'a, carrying a spring garden of a dish.
> It looks like it's dressed in robes of light.

Haroun's half-brother Ibrahim ibn al-Mahdi was amply rewarded by Caliph al-Amin for having brought such a superlative cook to Baghdad, while Bid'a herself reputedly received a neck-chain worth 300,000 silver dirhams.

✿ ✿ ✿ ✿ ✿ ✿ ✿ ✿ ✿ ✿ ✿ ✿ ✿ ✿ ✿ ✿ ✿

Sikbāj (modern version)

Cut 1 kilogram lamb shoulder into medium-sized cubes and place in a heavy casserole together with 25 grams of chopped fresh coriander, cinnamon and salt to taste. Cover with water and cook gently until the meat is almost tender. Cover with water and simmer for 45 minutes or until the meat is nearly tender. Remove any scum if necessary. Meanwhile chop 1 large onion finely and slice 450 grams of leeks (use only the white parts) diagonally into thin half-rounds. Peel and dice one small aubergine (about 225 grams), and sweat over a low heat in olive oil in a separate pan. Add the onion and leeks to the casserole and simmer for around 10 minutes before adding the aubergine pieces. Quickly dry-fry two teaspoons of whole coriander seeds and crush in a pestle and mortar or blitz briefly in a blender before adding them to the casserole. Cook for a further 20 minutes. In the meantime, mix 250 grams of white wine vinegar with a pinch of saffron strands and 1 tablespoon honey. Let the saffron steep in the liquid until it turns a golden-yellow colour, then add to the casserole. Take 50 grams each of dried, halved dates and figs, 25 grams of raisins that have been reflated in warm water and 50 grams of blanched almond halves and sprinkle them over the contents of the casserole. Cover and cook gently for a further 30 minutes. Finish the dish by pouring in a little lamb stock to loosen the mixture. To serve, carefully remove the top layer of dried fruit and almonds with a spoon and set aside, ladle the meat onto the centre of a large serving plate and surround it with the fruit and nuts. If so desired, you can garnish the meat with a small handful of lightly toasted pine kernels. For a finishing touch, sprinkle the dish with rosewater before serving.

This recipe for *sikbāj* is based on one devised by the chef Ian Fraser at the suggestion of David Waines. Emeritus Professor of Middle East and Islamic Studies at the University of Lancaster, Waines is one of the most original researchers into the culinary history of Islamic societies. He floated the idea to Ian Fraser of recreating Arab dishes from the Middle Ages in a modern guise.

In his book, *Cooking, Cuisine and Class. A Study in Comparative Sociology*, the British social anthropologist Jack Goody has pointed to the fact that, in addition to ingredients and recipes, the most essential prerequisite for the development of a significant cuisine is a large corpus of 'adventurous eaters'. It was not enough, Goody maintains, for a court and its foremost members to simply have the wherewithal to eat well. Rather, there also needed to be a large middle class consisting of officials, military officers, artists and merchants who were interested in adventuresome food and who were ready and able to spend the requisite funds in order to obtain it. This middle class developed very rapidly in the Abbasid empire. Indeed, generally speaking, Arab society of this period was characterised by a high degree of social mobility. Political upheavals could mean that a vizier suddenly found himself back in gaol once again, stripped of all his power and possessions. By contrast, a humble artisan, a simple scribe or a musician could find himself unexpectedly raised up to the elite by a stroke of good fortune. As a result of this social mobility, knowledge of good food and interesting ingredients spread throughout all classes. Above all, the criteria for culinary quality formed part of the general canon of knowledge from the 9th century onwards. Cooking, eating and drinking became favourite pastimes among many well-off people.

The activity of cooking was so well thought of that artists, intellectuals and even the caliphs themselves all tried their hand at it. However, they were not always so sure of their expertise in the kitchen. In such situations they were accustomed to roping in an experienced professional chef to help them out. In any event, we know of several poets and singers who were just as renowned for particular dishes as they were for their other artistic skills. For instance, it was said of the famous chanteuse Arib that an acquaintance once came upon her cooking three dishes simultaneously.

She was evidently a virtuosic talent when it came to culinary matters. Likewise, al-Mukharik (d. 844), the greatest poet and singer of his time, was reputed to be adept at preparing an excellent *harīsa*. Many other *harīsa* recipes from the Abbasid period are still known about today, though these should not be confused with the Tunisian spice paste of the same name (alternatively spelt 'harissa'). The name of the recipe derives from the Arabic word for 'to grind' or 'to crush'.

Harīsa with sugar

This recipe comes from the Arabian Peninsula.

Simmer I kilogram of lamb, chicken or beef on the bone, skimming the surface to removed unwanted scum. When the meat is soft, lift it out of the broth with a large slotted spoon, discard the bones and cut the meat into small pieces. Put the meat back into the pan with three cups of whole wheat grains and simmer for as long as it takes for the wheat grains to become completely soft. Finally add a little hot water. Remove from the heat and mash the stew with a wooden spoon until the wheat grains are fully crushed. Pour into a serving dish and sprinkle with a pinch each of sugar and ground cardamom, plus a dribble of butterfat and a small amount of either sugar or honey.

According to this basic principle, a *harīsa* can also be made from a stock containing half a chicken or other meat, to which whole wheat grains or wheat porridge has been added. After cooking, the stew is seasoned with salt and dried herbs and the wheat grains are mashed to a pulp.

The Caliph al-Muʻtasim (r. 833–842) took great delight in organising cooking competitions between his guests at some of his evening banquets. At the end, he would taste the individual dishes they had prepared and rate them. The person who had cooked the meal that pleased him best was rewarded with a special present. His predecessor as caliph, the historically important figure, al-Maʼmun (ruled 813–833), was by all accounts a very keen cook himself. It was reported that he once overseasoned a dish with musk, thereby rendering it inedible. It may be that he was trying to hint at his great wealth through his liberal use of this expensive ingredient, although this fact would have impressed itself upon the assembled company just as effectively if he had actually served them something palatable.

During the reign of the Abbasids, some of the most highly prized ingredients were imported ones. Nowadays, the vegetables and other ingredients in question form part of the basic repertoire of Middle Eastern and Mediterranean cuisine, for example the aubergine. This vegetable must surely have become known to the Arabs as early as the Muslim conquest of Iran, and yet it was still regarded as something quite exotic in the 9th century. Contemporary physicians were of the view that aubergines were unhealthy, and people generally found them too bitter. A Bedouin at the time supposedly described them in the following terms: 'Their colour is that of a scorpion's abdomen, and their taste is like its sting.' It clearly needed quite a bit of experimentation before people hit upon the fact that the bitter juices of the aubergine could be leached out by sprinkling the cut surfaces of the vegetable with salt.

On 23 December 825, Caliph al-Maʼmun married a young woman called Khadija, who had been given the nickname Buran, after a pre-Islamic Persian princess. She was the daughter of his former vizier, al-Hasan ibn Sahl. To mark the occasion, one of the most magnificent feasts that Baghdad had ever witnessed – or would ever see again – was held. In view of the great significance of the event, the aubergine dish that was served at this banquet was something quite out of the ordinary for its time. And yet from a modern perspective, all it consisted of was aubergines that had been salted and rinsed before being fried in oil. Some Arab authors claimed that Buran herself had invented this dish.

Hence its name – *būrāniyya*.

Over time, this aubergine recipe evolved, becoming ever more complicated. In Moorish Spain (al-Andalus), the aubergines for *būrāniyya* were sliced lengthways and hollowed out, and the flesh that had been scooped out was mixed with minced meat. This mixture was spooned back into the hollowed-out shell and the whole thing was then baked. The princess' name was even used later for similarly constructed dishes of squash with a meat filling. Nowadays, the terms *būrāni* or *būrāniyya* are still used in Syrian or Lebanese cuisine for vegetable dishes of this kind; they are also found in other countries throughout the Mediterranean, such as Turkey, Spain, Greece and the Balkan region.

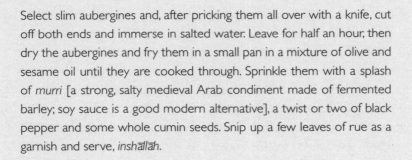

Būrāniyya

This recipe is taken from the Arab cookbook by Ibn Sayyar al-Warraq, *Annals of the Caliphs' Kitchens*, from 10th-century Baghdad.

Select slim aubergines and, after pricking them all over with a knife, cut off both ends and immerse in salted water. Leave for half an hour, then dry the aubergines and fry them in a small pan in a mixture of olive and sesame oil until they are cooked through. Sprinkle them with a splash of *murri* [a strong, salty medieval Arab condiment made of fermented barley; soy sauce is a good modern alternative], a twist or two of black pepper and some whole cumin seeds. Snip up a few leaves of rue as a garnish and serve, *inshāllāh*.

In an expanded version of this recipe from the same cookbook, walnuts, rue and coriander leaves are added to the aubergine:

Spread the cooked aubergine on a plate. While the dish is still warm, lay 20 fresh shelled and halved walnuts on top. Cover the plate with a clean cloth to allow the nuts to release their oil into the aubergines. To finish, slice some leek (white part only) along with some leaves of fresh rue and coriander and flash fry in a little olive oil before adding these to the dish.

The elites of the Abbasid caliphate could afford certain products that were beyond the reach of not only the common people but also the middle classes. In addition to top-quality meat and fish, it was above all the many expensive spices that constituted this class distinction. Ibrahim al-Mahdi, a prince of the Abbasid house, was not only a poet and a gifted musician but also an outstanding gourmet. In the upheavals that erupted over who should succeed his father, Caliph al-Mahdi, Ibrahim occupied this post for two years, from 815 to 817, although he was never really recognised as the legitimate caliph. When he was finally forced to abdicate, he was fortunate to escape with his life. Whether this was down to his beautiful singing or his culinary mastery or simply because he did not represent a political threat has not been recorded for posterity. However, his name has gone down in history through being associated with a very special dish in which minced meat is combined with whole pieces of meat, which he is believed to have invented:

Ibrahīmiyya

The following is a translation of the original recipe from the *Kitab al-Tabikh* of al-Katib al-Baghdadi from the 13th century.

Cut some lamb into medium-sized pieces, place it in a tagine and cover with water, adding salt to taste. Make up a small bouquet garni consisting of ground coriander and black pepper, finely chopped ginger, a couple of short cinnamon sticks and a piece of gum mastic; place all these in a small piece of muslin and tie the neck firmly. Add to the meat, along with some finely chopped onions. While this is cooking, form little meatballs from the minced lamb, add these to the other ingredients and continue cooking until everything is tender. Remove the bouquet garni at this point. Mix grape juice with finely ground almonds and water to make a thick paste. Taste it, and if the mixture is too bitter, sweeten with a little sugar. Tip this into the tagine as a thickening agent, and let the dish simmer for at least another hour on a slow heat. At the end of the cooking time, carefully wipe down the sides of the tagine with a clean, damp cloth, sprinkle some rosewater over the dish and – *inshallah* – serve immediately.

❧ ❧ ❧ ❧ ❧ ❧ ❧ ❧ ❧ ❧ ❧ ❧ ❧ ❧ ❧ ❧ ❧ ❧

Towards the end of Abbasid rule, outbreaks of political disorder also brought a deterioration in the culinary situation. In Mesopotamia, agricultural production was severely affected by clashes with Mongol invaders, while international trade was hampered by punitive tariffs. Besides, the general economic situation was beginning to suffer from increasing competition from the Spanish and the Portuguese, with the result that even the Mameluke rulers in Cairo were obliged to have their food ingredients bought from the city's bazaars. North African rulers began feuding with one another and at the same time found themselves confronted by the Christian kings of Spain, who had succeeded in bringing most of the Iberian Peninsula under their control by this time and expelling both Muslims and Jews in the process. These refugees had immediately found a new home on the far side of the Mediterranean; even today, part of the Moroccan city of Fez is still named the 'Andalusian quarter'. Sephardic Jews even fetched up in Thessaloniki in northern Greece, where they enriched the life and cuisine of the city until their deportation by the Nazis in the Second World War. Migrant Andalusian Muslims and Jews combined the elegance and refinement of Iberian cuisine with the traditions of North Africa and the Eastern Mediterranean. They also found a safe haven even further east under the protection of the newly founded Ottoman Empire.

The Ottomans

Further changes and advances in the cuisine of the Near and Middle East only become apparent with the rise and expansion of the Ottoman Empire into a major power. The empire was made up of several provinces with diverse climatic conditions and corresponding culinary traditions, ranging from those of Central Asia to those of the Arab provinces and the Balkans.

The network of roads between the various administrative centres was extensive and well maintained, while the steady increase in shipping along the major rivers and across the Mediterranean played a major part in keeping the populace under Ottoman rule well supplied. In the main, the provision of foodstuffs was secure. Right up to the 17th century, Ottoman bureaucracy was renowned throughout Europe as exemplary. This was due to the fact that administrative officials were selected on the basis of how good they were at the job. Unlike in the Christian West at that time, no account was taken of aristocratic background in a person's advancement. The great court kitchens of the empire were organised along the same lines. Indeed, there was a positively bureaucratic system governing the kitchens at the court of the Ottoman Sultan. Over a thousand servants were employed there. One of the kitchens was devoted solely to preparing food for the Sultan, and another for the Sultan's mother. Above all, aside from the royal household and inner circle of courtiers, the entire staff of the Ottoman court had to be fed, and they numbered in their thousands. Catering took place according to the various ranks of officials.

We know about the great diversity of dishes that were cooked and eaten at the Ottoman Sultan's court thanks to the extensive records kept by the 'victualling departments'. These records meticulously itemise the enormous variety of foodstuffs, the quantities supplied and the costs incurred. At the Ottoman court, as an institutionalised procedure dining primarily formed part of the duties of the higher ranks of the bureaucracy. The table talk that was conducted on such occasions proved to be less noteworthy, despite the fact that these mealtimes would have provided an informal forum for discussing the political or technical administrative questions arising from foregoing negotiations. The true significance of these meals, which ultimately were held at the invitation of the ruler, was to demonstrate the ministers' and provincial governors' dependence upon the Sultan. Accordingly, after cabinet meetings, viziers were offered sumptuous meals consisting of up to six separate courses. The menu began traditionally with a rice dish, followed by a chicken soup. Next came various dishes that were typical of Ottoman cuisine, like *dolma* or *börek*, savoury preparations of either meat or vegetables wrapped in vine leaves or different types of pastry and oven-baked. These were followed by sweets, such as various types of baklava. The menu concluded with the main meat course, which usually comprised *köfte* (meatballs) prepared in many different ways, each with its own name, or alternatively kebabs. The Sultan also had up to a thousand meals a day distributed to the populace of Istanbul. These would doubtless have been less elaborate affairs; at least there are no accounts of luxury dishes in this context.

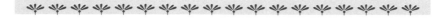

Kadinbudu köfte ('Women's thighs koftas')

Bring to the boil 125 millilitres of lightly salted water and tip in a handful of rice; simmer gently until cooked and then drain and leave to stand. In the meantime, take a large onion that has been finely chopped and sweat it in butter until translucent. Add the drained rice and cook with the onion until any residual moisture has evaporated. In a separate frying pan or skillet, fry a portion of minced lamb until brown. Then combine this with an equal quantity of raw minced lamb, the rice-onion mixture, salt, pepper, cinnamon and 1 beaten raw egg. Knead together for several minutes and then, using your palms, form into balls roughly the size of hen's eggs, flattening them out slightly at the end of the rolling process. Finally roll them in seasoned flour or dip in beaten egg and coat with breadcrumbs, and fry in a shallow layer of oil, turning once, until both sides are nicely browned. Take the pan off the heat but leave the lid on and let the koftas stand for 5 minutes to continue warming through in their own steam. Before serving they can be sprinkled with a little ground cinnamon if desired.

Some *köfte* recipes specify the addition of finely chopped parsley or a spice mix made from various different kinds of pepper, cumin, dried mint and oregano. The individuality of each variation comes in the use of different types of mince meat cooked in slightly different ways.

Especially on the occasion of major celebrations, such as the circumcision of a prince, a practice referred to in the historical records as *yagma* ('pillage') was rife; it is thought to have been based on Central Asian models. The 'leftovers from the gathering', which remained uneaten from the excessive quantities of food that were served up at dinners for the political leadership, were donated to the guards of the elite force of Janissaries that guarded the Sultan. The soldiers would eagerly jostle and fight among themselves as they took possession of the leftovers. In later periods, such occasions became something of a ritual. The Grand Vizier would first seek the Sultan's permission before the troops were allowed to fall upon the waiting food and devour it. At these feasts, no fewer than 200 boiled and 300 roasted sheep were served; each sheep contained a live dove, which was released and fluttered off when the carcass was carved open. In addition, there were 4,500 platters of rice. In spite of the discipline that prevailed at the Ottoman court, these occasions often became rowdy. After one such ritual 'pillage' in the city of Edirne in 1715, not only had all the food vanished but also 56 valuable copper cooking vessels, many of which had only been borrowed for the feast. The Nuremberg orientalist Salomon Schweigger, who in 1577 was a member of an Austrian delegation to the 'Sublime Porte' (the Ottoman court) reported in amazement: 'No sooner had we risen from our places at table than the Janissary bodyguards and other courtly people of their ilk fell upon the leftovers with the same voracity shown by vultures and raptors when swooping on their prey. Yet while we found the sight of them banqueting in this way quite repellent (as I said to one of our number: "In Germany, you'd find more decorum at a country fair!"), they clearly considered it a noble and imperial feast. And so they snatched and carried off every last morsel that was there – it is a truly yokelish and clumsy courtly manner that does not bridle at such barbarities.'

Yet it was not only the officials who were employed directly at the Sublime Porte who were fed by the Sultan's kitchens but also all the Sultan's subjects who had anything whatsoever to do with the Ottoman court. Meat played an important role, since its consumption was regarded as particularly prestigious and it was correspondingly expensive; it was distributed in the town on the occasion of special feast days. The gardens that were located in the environs of Istanbul, with large areas set aside for the production of fruit and vegetables, not only supplied the court but also fed the entire populace of the city.

However, as the city grew over time, the quantities of food harvested from these market gardens would surely not have been enough to feed everyone. In any event, it is on record that the Sultan's kitchen processed no fewer than forty different varieties of aubergine that came from the imperial market gardens.

Generally speaking, the court of the Sultan acted as a model for the elites of the Ottoman Empire. Its cultural standards set the tone not least in the realm of cookery. Even at the homes of wealthy Ottoman Turks who were not employed at the court, menus comprising several courses were served, with each course involving the most elaborate combination of different foods. An integral part of this complexity involved preparing meat in three different ways: sweet, sour and normal. A meal in a prosperous Ottoman household might comprise onions or courgettes with a meat filling, stuffed vine leaves, spinach, rice dishes cooked in several ways, various types of *börek*, and desserts made either from fruits or the inevitable array of different sorts of baklava. Of course, many dishes typical of particular regions were also devised. But over time, a common culinary canon developed that one might justifiably term 'Ottoman cuisine'.

The Safavids

Many historians trace the origins of modern Persian (Iranian) cuisine directly back to the dynasty and the court of the Safavids, who ruled the country from 1501 to 1722. It is certainly the case that, during this dynasty's more than two-hundred-year long rule, a complex culinary culture evolved both at the royal court at Isfahan and among the wealthy resident populace of this magnificent showpiece city. Members of the Safavid elite were responsible for the rediscovery of rice. This staple had been known about in Iran in pre-Islamic times, but had since fallen into desuetude because it was not greatly to the taste of the Arab conquerors. Instead, bread became established as the true staple diet of most Persians. Under the Safavids, however, people once more began devising more sophisticated ways of preparing and serving rice, gradually turning this aptitude into a fine art. To the present day, rice prepared in the Persian manner, which is known as *polo*, must be served with its grains separate and light and bearing no resemblance to the sticky or glutinous forms of rice prevalent in the Far East.

People discovered that these dishes could be made more flavoursome through the addition of herbs or the expensive crocus-stigma-derived spice of saffron. At around the same time, Iran was the location of the first combinations of rice and fruit, now a characteristic trait of Persian cuisine.

Polo barreh (Lamb with rice)

Because no original cookbooks from the Safavid period have been found to date, this recipe dates from the successor dynasty of the Qajars (1779–1925):

Cut a large piece of lamb (shoulder or leg) into small pieces and put them in a suitably large cooking vessel. For a presentation meal, one should use a dainty, well-fattened suckling lamb; also add a good amount of softened chickpeas that have been squeezed by hand from their outer husks without squashing them. Then add 20 *methqāl* (c. 80 grams) of best-quality cinnamon bark, along with 10 *methqāl* root ginger cut into large chunks and the same quantity each of ground black pepper, ground cardamom and cloves. All these ingredients should be cooked with a quantity of roasted finely sliced onion and white rice that has been carefully picked over to remove any impurities. On no account should the rice grains be broken. If you happen to have to hand any marrow from hollow bones, add this to the pot as well. It is essential to cook this dish in a single step; be sure to only add the aforementioned rice, well washed, once the meat has reached a soft consistency. As soon as the dish has reached simmering point again after the addition of the rice, sprinkle it with another generous portion of finely sliced onion and 5 *methqāl* (c. 20 grams) of *kermani zireh* (wild black Persian cumin) together with an appropriate amount of salt and oil. Put the lid on the pot and create a tight closure by sealing the rim with dough. Heap up red-hot glowing charcoal around the base of the pot. After an hour, break open the dough seal, open the lid – and truly bear witness to Allah's omnipotence. It is also entirely fitting to add little lamb meatballs to this dish if you so wish.

※ ※ ※ ※ ※ ※ ※ ※ ※ ※ ※ ※ ※ ※ ※ ※ ※

An especial favourite in Persian cuisine were the various kinds of sherbets. The Safavid court in Isfahan had a specially dedicated place for storing these, as described by the German traveller Engelbert Kämpfer (1651–1716), who visited the city in 1684: 'The court sherbet cellar is under the control of the court sherbet master, who oversees the manufacture of sherbets. By "sherbet" the Persians mean a cold drink made from water, sugar, the juice of tropical fruits and a splash of rosewater… Throughout the court sherbet cellar, not only were the constituent ingredients in the preparation of the drinks stored but also a whole range of essences, roots and fruit, some of them crystallised and some pickled in vinegar, along with all manner of made-up drinks, either ready to consume or in the form of viscous cordials.' Modern Iranian cookery is still characterised by diverse forms of rice dish as well as many different sorts of sherbet and sorbet. Clearly, the tradition of these preparations did not remain confined to the upper echelons of Iranian society.

※ ※ ※ ※ ※ ※ ※ ※ ※ ※ ※ ※ ※ ※ ※ ※ ※

Pomegranate and orange sorbet

The combination of pomegranate and orange juice is widespread in Iranian dishes. This particular method of preparation comes from a famous restaurant in Isfahan.

In a heavy-based pan, slowly heat up 250 millilitres of cold water mixed with 250 grams of icing sugar until the sugar has completely dissolved.

Bring to the boil and simmer for 1 minute. Remove the pan from the heat and allow to cool slightly. Pour 250 millilitres of freshly squeezed orange juice and 150 millilitres of pomegranate juice into the warm sugar syrup and mix thoroughly. Crush a few threads of saffron, soak them in warm water and add to the syrup and juice. Also add a few freshly ground cardamom seeds. Allow the mix to completely cool in the fridge. Finally, churn in an ice-cream maker according to the manufacturer's instructions. The finished sorbet can be kept for up to three days in a plastic tub with a lid in a deep freeze before eating.

The Mughal emperors

Both the cuisine and the rituals associated with the Muslim courts of India were conditioned by a combination of Persian, Central Asian and indigenous Indian elements. The Moroccan world traveller, Ibn Battuta, who visited the court of the Sultans of Delhi in the 14th century, reported that official banquets began with guests being served sugar-water perfumed with rosewater. A great succession of dishes then followed. The meal ended with the chewing of betel nuts and leaves. A particular favourite dish was *samūsak*, which is known in the cuisines of the Middle East under the very similar name of *sambūsak*. It is one of a number of dishes which involve mixing together finely minced meat with pistachios, almonds, walnuts, onions and various spices and quickly frying this mixture before wrapping it in thinly rolled pastry, brushing it with ghee (clarified butter) or oil and baking it in the oven. Indian aristocrats were in the habit of feeding their entire administrative apparatus at midday. Evidently, no expense was spared at these communal lunches. Good bread, goat meat, chickens and rice dishes were served. Drinks included a kind of beer and sugared water. At the end of the meal, betel leaves were passed around. If any leftovers remained, they were handed out to the poor.

The destruction of the Delhi Sultanate by the Mongol conqueror Timur the Lame in 1398 saw the emergence of a series of small Muslim states; the most extraordinary of these was Mandu in Central India, under the rulership of

Ghiyath Shahi (15th–16th century). On his accession to the throne, the Sultan announced that he intended to fight no wars but instead to devote himself entirely to pleasure, in which his people should also participate. Subsequently, the only name by which people referred to the capital city of Mandu was Shadiyabad ('City of Joy'). The Sultan installed his son as his successor, while he was still alive, to run the actual affairs of state. Ghiyath Shahi kept an enormous harem of female slaves. Tradition has it that they numbered as many as 16,000. The cleverest of these women received an education. They learned how to dance, sing, and play a musical instrument and how to read aloud and recite poetry.

In order that the Sultan might continue to fund his hedonistic lifestyle others were instructed in the practices of administration and accounting so that they were in a position to run successful manufactories. It was with these women that Ghiyath Shahi spent his lunchtimes. In addition, he raised an army of 500 Abyssinian slave women, who bore arms and were well-drilled in the use of swords and shields. He attracted several poets, painters of miniatures and calligraphers to his court. Not least, chefs were also an important part of his entourage; as a cookbook of the period, decorated with miniatures, demonstrates, these chefs were very inventive and devised several new recipes.

The rulers of the later Mughal dynasty originally came from Central Asia. Babur (d. 1530), the founder of the dynasty, did not enjoy Indian food, preferring Turkish cuisine instead. His successor Humayun (d. 1556) showed absolutely no interest in the art of cookery. It was only with the accession of the Mughal emperor Akbar the Great (r. 1556–1605) and his two successors Jahangir (r. 1605–1627) and Shah Jahan (r. 1627–1658) that a premium was once again placed on good food. Naturally, the influence of Turkish and Persian cuisine remained clearly in evidence at the Mughal court. Yet the vegetarian doctrines of Hinduism also began increasingly to make their mark on the Muslim elite in India. It was reported of the Mughal emperor Akbar that he only very rarely ate meat. According to an account given by the Spanish Jesuit missionary Antonio Monserrate in 1580, Akbar refrained from eating meat every Friday, every Sunday, on every first day of the month of the solar year, throughout the entire month of Farwardin (late March to late April) and also that of Aban (late October to late November) – the month in which he was born. The umbrella term applied to the dishes that he ate instead on these occasions was *safiyāna,* which comes from the Arabic word for 'pure'. Clearly the Jesuit priest was particularly impressed by the similarity between Akbar's observances and the fasting rules of Western Christianity. Unfortunately, though, Monserrate tells us nothing about the Muslim fasting practices at the court of Akbar the Great.

Furthermore, Akbar was wont to eat only one meal a day; certainly, we know that there was no set mealtime. Consequently, the kitchen had to be at a permanent state of readiness. As soon as the ruler felt pangs of hunger, a hundred different dishes had to be prepared and served within an hour.

The significance of food in Mughal society was explained by the contemporary historiographer Abul Fazl: 'The balance of human nature, a person's physical strength, their ability to assimilate external and internal aptitudes, and the acquisition of worldly and religious assets all depend on the final analysis upon the proper care being taken, as shown in the selection of appropriate food. This knowledge is what separates human beings from animals.' Under Akbar's rule, at least, beef and veal were not cooked in the court kitchens. This may have been because of the sanctity of this animal in Hinduism. But it was also found only very rarely on medieval Arab or Persian bills of fare. By contrast, rice dishes comprised all the more important an element of Mughal cuisine. As in Iran, virtually a cult was created in Mughal India out of preparing food. Despite India's greater proximity to the most important sources of spices, however, these played only a subsidiary role in the refinement of dishes. In any event, there are records of pepper, cardamom, coriander seeds, cinnamon, cloves and fresh root ginger being used; there is no mention, though, of any stronger Southern Indian spices. Great store was set by vegetables and fruit. The Mughal court maintained extensive market gardens and orchards growing the most diverse assortment of fruits and vegetables. Particular attention was paid to the keeping and raising of poultry destined for the imperial table. These birds were not only fed by hand, they were also given breadcrumbs steeped in saffron and rosewater. In addition, they were massaged daily with oil and musk. Poultry-based dishes for the Mughal emperors were often highly complex affairs, though some recipes have survived to the present day in the Indo-Muslim culinary tradition. Examples of such dishes include *murgh musallam* (a deboned chicken stuffed with rice and herbs) and the ubiquitous biryani (a rice dish mixed with meat, fish or egg).

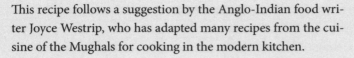

Biryani

This recipe follows a suggestion by the Anglo-Indian food writer Joyce Westrip, who has adapted many recipes from the cuisine of the Mughals for cooking in the modern kitchen.

Take 1 kilogram of boned lamb meat (shoulder or leg) and cut it into cubes each measuring roughly 2 centimetres square. Peel 2 large onions and slice thinly. In a large pan, heat 4 tablespoons ghee (or butter) and fry the onions until golden brown. Meanwhile, skin and crush 2 plump garlic cloves; peel and finely chop a generous cube of root ginger and mix with the garlic before adding to the frying onions. At the same time, add the meat to the pan and brown well on all sides. Now season and spice the dish with 5 cloves, 1 teaspoon cardamom powder, 2 small pieces of cinnamon bark, a quarter to half a teaspoon ground turmeric, a pinch of chili powder, 200 grams of plain yoghurt, 100 millilitres of lamb stock and salt to taste. Cook over a gentle heat for 40 minutes, stirring occasionally. Towards the end of the cooking time, thoroughly wash and drain around 250 grams basmati rice. Put the rice in a saucepan barely covered with water, bring to the boil and simmer over medium heat for 5 minutes. Meanwhile, pre-heat the oven to a medium temperature, 180°C (fan-assisted 150°C/ gas mark 4). Decant the cooked lamb mixture into an overproof dish with a lid. Drain the boiled rice and heap on top of the meat, then seal the lid tightly. Leave in the oven for an hour. Just before serving, in a dry skillet quickly flash-fry a handful of pistachio kernels and a handful of blanched whole almonds, and sprinkle 50 grams of raisins with rosewater. Serve the meat and rice onto plates and garnish with the nut and dried fruit mix.

From the various sources relating to the history of the Mughal Empire it becomes abundantly clear that its rulers lived in permanent fear of being poisoned by dishes that were served to them. Every conceivable security measure was taken to guard against this. For example, the historian Abul Fazl reported that: 'When meals are being prepared and dishes being sent out from the kitchen, a screen is erected and spectators are kept at a distance. The cooks roll up their sleeves and pull up the hems of their garments to keep them out of the way and hold their hands in front of their noses and mouths when the dishes are carried out of the kitchen. The head chef and the first overseer taste the dishes. Then they are tasted for a second time by the principal overseer before being decanted into individual serving dishes.

The gold and silver platters are wrapped in red cloths, while the dishes made of copper and porcelain are wrapped in white cloths. The principal overseer closes the dishes with his seal and notes on it the exact contents of each dish. The scribe in the serving antechamber then draws up a list of all the dishes and meals that he has been delivered and dispatches it into the innermost regions of the court; this list is also sealed by the principal overseer to avoid individual dishes getting mixed up. The dishes are then carried in by the first overseers, the cooks, and other servants, preceded and followed by teams of sceptre-bearers, who are there to ensure that no unauthorised persons approach the dishes. At the same time, the servants from the serving antechamber despatch baskets sealed by the principal overseer. These contain various sorts of bread, stacks of small bowls with types of fermented milk in them, slim stands supporting platters of pickled vegetables, fresh ginger, limes, and various different green leaves. The servants of the inner palace once again taste the meals in their turn, then spread a large white cloth on the ground and arrange the dishes on it. When, after a while, the emperor duly begins eating, the servants sit opposite him, ready to pass him the next dish. The first thing to happen when His Majesty starts the meal with milk and milk products is to set aside a portion of these for the dervishes. When the emperor has dined, he prostrates himself in prayer. The principal overseer is in constant attendance throughout. The dishes are taken away in the order stipulated on the aforementioned list. However, a few dishes are kept back and warmed through in the event that they might still be required.'

The beginning of the colonial period saw both Muslim culinary practices and the broad palette of different dishes expand in all regions of the Islamic world. Even so the basic structures of ambitious Islamic cuisine remained intact from North Africa to the Indian Subcontinent: vegetables, rice and bread were its key elements, while meat was of lesser importance. Ready-cooked or half-prepared dishes – above all in the desserts line – that were produced in bazaars, also continued in widespread use.

Cookbooks and Kitchen Practices

The preparation of food and drink, unlike the practice of the fine arts, architecture or craftsmanship, can only be handed down through exposition, be this either in written form or sometimes also with the aid of images. Transmissions of this kind can be found in great abundance in the literatures of the Near and Middle East, and can be readily consulted: over the past few decades, a large number of medieval cookbooks and sources on the cultural history of food have been published. Whereas direct information about what exactly went on in cooking pots may be gleaned primarily from Arabic cookbooks, insights into the people who cooked it must be pieced together from the extensive body of historical, literary and other accounts.

Professional chefs

Any sophisticated cuisine demands competent cooks. In the different regions of the Islamic world, professional cooks played a key role in the development of the Muslim culinary arts. They were to be found in all social classes. Among the powerful, prominent and wealthy, kitchens were perfectly and meticulously organised, each according to the size of the household in question and the number of people who needed to be catered for. Meanwhile, in smaller households there was, as a general rule, only a single cook, male or female, sometimes supported by an assistant. These helpers, but also the cooks themselves, could be either slaves or free men and women. The most important of the cooks' many tasks was to obtain provisions for the household; for this they were supplied with an appropriate budget. Slaves and free men and women alike had the financial wherewithal to acquire cooking ingredients and also to buy in sufficient firewood or other forms of fuel.

In Muslim households, even the domestic slaves enjoyed a high degree of independence. They were permitted to undertake business trips on behalf of their masters and to this end were furnished with the necessary funds.

Even cooks in smaller households were required to have a broad repertoire of recipes at their fingertips in order to meet the demands of their masters. They were called upon to demonstrate their skills particularly when unexpected guests were present at table. It was impossible for these chefs to specialise in particular kinds of preparation or individual dishes. In the case of households that set great store by the food that was served, numerous consultations had to take place and so a close rapport would often develop between those who ran the household and the kitchen staff. Such closeness did not, of course, rule out conflicts, should the result of the endeavours in the kitchen not come up to the expectations of the master and mistress of the house.

By contrast, the large households of the elites required a sizeable personnel working in the kitchen. Of necessity, this gave rise to a rigidly structured hierarchy of roles within the kitchen. From the accounts written by contemporary historians and travellers, it is possible to learn a great deal about the organisation of the kitchens at royal courts but also about the ways in which monastery and army field kitchens were organised. Astonishingly, it transpires that no structural divergences of note existed between these various types of kitchen, although their size varied considerably. At the head of the kitchen brigade stood a figure known as the *sāhib al-matbakh* (the chief administrator, literally 'master of the kitchen'). His duties included ensuring that the kitchen operated economically and the cooks did not overspend on the budget that was allocated to them. If such an administrator was shrewd and successful, this might well smooth his path to promotion to more senior positions in the running of the royal household, or even of the state, as demonstrated by the biography of the later vizier of the Abbasid Caliph al-Mutaʿsim (r. 833–842), al-Fadl ibn Marwan (774–864). His first role was that of *sāhib al-matbakh*, from which he steadily rose until he came to occupy some of the highest offices of the state. Yet it was perfectly possible even for others working in the court kitchen who showed dedication in preparing exquisite dishes for the ruler's table to find favour with their masters.

The Mughal rulers in particular, who attached great importance to the quality of the food that was presented to them, were often very well disposed towards their chefs and treated them with manifest respect. The historical accounts make it clear that even the cooks who worked at the kitchen of the court at Delhi could earn great prestige and influence. For it was no easy task organising a major court kitchen. At the royal seats of Baghdad or Delhi, of Córdoba or Istanbul, the requirement was that all the dishes known from the Islamic culinary tradition should, where possible, be kept pretty much on tap for the ruler and his guests to enjoy. Immediately beneath the chief administrator stood the head chef (*ustādh*, or 'master'), who was in charge of the kitchen brigade (*tabbākh*, 'cooks'). The lowliest members of the kitchen hierarchy were the trainee cooks (*tilmīdh*, 'pupils').

The costs incurred by a court kitchen could be quite considerable. The budget drawn up by the Abbasid caliph al-Mu'tadid (r. 892–902) set aside 1,500 dinars a month just for the wages of the cooks employed in his kitchen; this sum did not include the costs of auxiliaries like water bearers or fire stokers. During the reign of this particular caliph, which saw a steep rise in the cost of living, a 60 kilogram sack of grain cost one dinar. In other words, the wage bill for the cooks alone could have bought 90,000 kilograms of wheat. Alongside the official wages paid, there was also an indirect form of recompense, in that the cooks were allowed to sell off the surplus ingredients that had not been needed in the preparation of generally very lavish dishes and pocket the proceeds themselves. These generally included the less exalted cuts of meat like the heads, the feet and the offal. Vegetables and fruit that no longer met the royal court's exacting standards could also be sold for profit. It is not known how, or whether, this income was distributed among the kitchen staff. As a general rule, the cooks were allowed to eat the dishes that came back from the tables of the ruler and his entourage. Many a contemporary commentator complains that the cooks had already eaten the choicest parts of the meal even before the food was served.

Of course, this misbehaviour of theirs could never be proved as the *corpora delicti* had already disappeared. All the same, they were suspected of salting away some of the fattiest morsels for themselves. In the medieval Arab world, fat was regarded as particularly tasty, and commanded a high price. Accordingly, the chefs were suspected of having skimmed off and consumed the chicken fat whenever a bird was served very well-done. An exquisite chicken dish was served at the court of the Abbasid caliphs in Baghdad.

Shaljamiya (modern version)

Shaljam, is an Arabised word from the Persian *shalgham*, meaning 'turnip' or 'swede'. This recipe follows the modern adaptation by Ian Fraser of a medieval recipe by Ibrahim ibn al-Mahdi. In his book *In a Caliph's Kitchen: Mediaeval Arabic Cooking for the Modern Gourmet* (1989), Professor David Waines translated the original recipe from the earliest extant Arabic culinary work of Ibn Sayyar al-Warraq.

Set the oven at 200°C (gas mark 6). Take 675 grams of raw, boned chicken (half breast meat and half thigh meat, cut into 1 centimetre-wide strips) and fry in hot oil, then add a can (200 grams) pre-cooked chickpeas, washed and drained, and 75 grams of chopped spring onions and simmer for 30 minutes. Peel 450 grams of white turnip or swede, dice into small pieces and simmer in vegetable stock until tender; drain and mash finely or liquidise. In a mixer, or using a hand blender, make a smooth purée consisting of 4 egg whites, 50 grams of ground almonds and 75 grams of fresh soft goat's cheese or feta (ewe's milk cheese). After the chicken has simmered for 30 minutes, season with salt and pepper to taste and add a little ground cumin and sumac, plus 1 tablespoon Dijon mustard. Also add the turnip/swede purée at this stage and mix in thoroughly before turning into an ovenproof dish. Carefully spoon the egg, almond and cheese paste on top of the chicken mixture and spread evenly over the surface. Bake for 30 minutes. The paste will become a delicious crust which should be allowed to brown slightly in the oven. Serve garnished with a little chopped coriander or flat-leaf parsley.

Written accounts of kitchens of this period, at least those at royal courts, tell of cooks being required to remain constantly at their posts for the entire day and part of the night. If their workload permitted, they used any free time for personal pleasures.

Thus, we learn that on occasion the kitchen staff would invite one of the singers who frequently came to perform at court to sing for them so that they could marvel at his artistry.

Aside from the amount of money spent on ingredients, soup kitchens for the poor did not differ markedly in their basic structure from the court kitchens. They were funded by 'pious endowments' (Arabic *waqf*, plural *auqāf*). The advantage of these endowments was that, even though potential heirs of the original benefactors might ultimately profit from them, they were protected from being confiscated by state intervention by the provisions of Sharia law. These endowments were established by wealthy people primarily for the purpose of publicly demonstrating their piety. The finances themselves generally derived from the rents received for properties such as farms, mills or bazaar stalls. The rental charge was set, as were the wages of the cooks employed in the soup kitchens and the bill of fare served there. Egyptian certificates of endowments from the 16th century instruct those running soup kitchens to offer daily changing menus that should ideally contain meat. Furthermore, special meals should also be served on feast days; in this context, there was specific mention of rice with expensive ingredients like pepper and butter.

The young trainee chefs gained instruction in the culinary arts from their senior colleagues according to the principle of 'learning by doing'. Often, the actual or fabricated history of a recipe for a particular dish would play a key role in the transmission of theoretical knowledge and practical skills. This was especially true in the case of dishes with names that were not self-evident, such as *khushtabiya*. This name was held to originate from the following story: a Persian ruler once had an Arab cook, whom he took with him on his travels. Whenever the ruler entered his camp, he would tell the cook: '*gusht biyar!*' ('Bring me meat!'). The cook had already prepared some pieces of meat, grilled or boiled. In addition, he provided a sauce in which to dunk the meat. One day, the ruler arrived back at camp prematurely. Although the cook had already cut the meat up into pieces, he had not even got around to lighting the fire, let alone cooking the food. Some improvisation was urgently called for. So, he put the meat in a frying pan, poured some oil over it, sprinkled it with a little water and salt, added a finely chopped onion and pinches of some finely ground spices. He then covered the dish with an inverted bowl and lit a roaring fire so the meat would sear really quickly. The result was a really tasty dish with a simple sauce consisting of oil, meat juices and spices. The ruler was so pleased with it that it became his favourite dish. Hence the name *khushtabiya*.

As this story shows, the lives of court cooks were fraught with uncertainties and even risks. The frequently long routes from the palace kitchens to the dining rooms presented numerous opportunities for someone to poison the ruler's food. Of course the dishes' ultimate point of origin was the kitchen and hence the cooks themselves. The dishes were therefore tested by tasters, often several times over, as they made their way to the ruler's table. Even so, if a dish disagreed with the ruler, it was the chef who was naturally held responsible. The sources report that things tended to end badly for cooks whenever such incidents occurred. If rulers even got so much as an inkling that a cook was responsible for the failure of a particular dish, the outcome was potentially the cook's execution. Or the cook responsible had one of his hands summarily cut off, a punishment that Islamic law actually reserved for theft.

Hardly anything is known about the organisation of catering for the military institutions of the various armies of the Middle East. A few hints are given in the descriptions of the Janissary units of the Ottoman Empire. These troop contingents made up of slaves were paid no wages but rather received symbolic gifts of money, but they were housed and fed by the state. Accordingly, kitchen utensils and titles and ranks deriving from the culinary realm played an important role among these troops. Janissary commanders were known as *shorbāshi bashi* ('soup masters'), and their badges of rank portrayed crossed spoons. When they went on campaign they took with them a set of large ladles and a huge soup tureen. If this tureen was ever tipped over, this was held to signify that the unit was refusing to obey the Sultan's orders.

These units of several tens of thousands of soldiers apiece were composed of men who as children or youths had been taken into Ottoman service through the general levy of young boys in the empire known as the *devşirme* system. The boys were transported – in some cases forcibly but in others with the acquiescence of their usually Christian parents – to Istanbul, where they were earmarked for either the military or the bureaucracy according to their talents and physical constitution. Some learned how to tend and supervise the many great gardens belonging to the Sultan, while others became cooks at court. In the Janissary units, the boys were employed in many different roles. Some were sent to the kitchens, while others were assigned to look after the cattle herds that the Janissaries took with them on military operations in order to feed themselves. In their barracks, Janissary troops of course had at their disposal kitchens and provisions stores which they managed themselves. Some of their provisions like bread, meat or the winter beverage *bouza* (a drink made from fermented barley) were supplied from outside the barracks by their respective producers. The provisioning of troops was a complex logistical task that called for the deployment of a large personnel with diverse areas of expertise.

The largest group of professional chefs comprised those cooks who had chosen to specialise in making particular individual kinds of food, which they then offered for sale at the bazaars. Customers could take these dishes home with them and consume them there. Such bazaar cooks still exist today, and they make a major contribution to providing the urban populations with food. Some traditional bazaar cooks would prepare a single meat dish or related dishes which can be made at the same time using a common set of basic ingredients. Others offered appropriate side dishes. An astonishing differentiation between culinary products could be seen precisely in the milieu of these bazaar cookshops. For instance, among bakers, there was on the one hand the *khabbāz*, who made khubz or flatbreads, while on the other there was the *khamīrī*, the pastry cook, and the *kaʿkī*, who produced cakes. Meat was roasted by *shawwā*, while the *khallāl* sold not only different types of vinegar but also the popular vinegar-pickled vegetables. Meanwhile, the *bawārādī* offered various savoury and other appetisers, and the *kamūkhī* sold the roasted meat of lambs or goat kids.

Above all, though, the markets were home to a huge array of sellers of sweetmeats, whose manufacture required not only considerable experience but often also special containers and utensils. The *zalabāni* made a kind of pancake, the *lawwāz* (whose name derived from the Arabic word *lauz* for almond) produced a sweet made of almonds while the *halwāni* made the renowned *halwiyāt* or *halāwat* (halva) – a confection made from sesame paste (tahini) and sugar.

✳ ✳ ✳ ✳ ✳ ✳ ✳ ✳ ✳ ✳ ✳ ✳ ✳ ✳ ✳ ✳ ✳ ✳

Halāwat al-tumūr

This dish is based on archetypes from the ancient Middle East, and was described in Arabic cookbooks of the Middle Ages. Many different varieties of it are still made in Iraq and on the Arabian Peninsula.

In a heavy-based pan, dry-roast 200 grams of wheat flour. Once it has started to take on colour and release an aroma, cook gently for a further 5 minutes, then tip the flour into a bowl. In the same cooking pan, using a wooden spoon, crush and break up 500 grams of stoned dates (if you can, remove their skins as well) in 100 grams of melted butter over a medium heat. Gradually add the roasted flour to the crushed dates and stir well to mix. Add 1 teaspoon each of ground cardamom, ground fennel seeds, ground coriander seeds and powdered cinnamon, plus 1 tablespoon rosewater. Mix together thoroughly and bring all the ingredients together in a ball. If the mix is too firm at this point, pour in a splash of warm water to loosen slightly until it becomes easier to work once more. Spread the mixture out onto a clean baking tray and smooth the surface with a palette knife. Decorate with roasted whole almonds, pine kernels and walnuts. Allow to cool before cutting into individual squares.

✲ ✲ ✲ ✲ ✲ ✲ ✲ ✲ ✲ ✲ ✲ ✲ ✲ ✲ ✲ ✲ ✲ ✲

Some of the vendors from the bazaar cookshops peddled their soups and stews around the streets, advertising the quality of their wares with loud street cries. Even today, the alleyways of the working-class districts of Cairo are home to street vendors of a thick bean stew (*Ful mudammas*), which is sold above all as warm and hearty breakfast fare. It is made from broad beans, lentils, tomatoes, onions, lemon juice, chili powder, ground cumin, salt and pepper, and is garnished with a mixture of chopped fresh tomatoes, chopped green peppers and finely shredded green salad leaves. There were also other cooks who sold their products from fixed locations. These were dishes that it would have been impractical to hawk on the streets without more ado, because they had for example to be weighed out more precisely or to ideally have the finishing touches put to them immediately before they were sold; or because technical implements that were not transportable were involved in making them – this applied particularly to bakeries and purveyors of roast meat. These foods, in common with all other products in the bazaar, were regulated by a market supervisory body. The senior bailiff of the market (*muhtasib*) had the power to impose on-the-spot fines for infringements of the rules. The list of punishments ranged from exclusion from the market via fines and the confiscation of equipment or goods to corporal punishments such as a set number of strokes of the lash. For the immediate imposition of physical punishments, the market bailiff used his slippers. However, given the multiplicity of products that were offered for sale at a Middle Eastern market, it was not always possible for the bailiffs to discover counterfeit foodstuffs. To assist them in their appraisal they used handbooks (*kutub al-hisba*) containing guidelines on how to judge the freshness of prepared foods or how to tell whether expensive commodities like saffron had been adulterated with additives such as turmeric or even sand. Such methods of falsification were also known in the West, where for example unscrupulous traders would bulk out black peppercorns with tiny balls of lead shot.

These manuals also contained rules on how to set up production facilities and maintain hygienic conditions; these regulations bear a striking resemblance to modern Western norms in such matters. For instance, the minimum height of bakery chimneys was stipulated in order to minimise the risk of fire.

In addition, bakers were instructed to wear sleeveless tops and a face mask when kneading bread dough. To prevent sweat from dripping into the dough, a headband was also recommended. Bakers' heads were to be shaved so that no hair dropped into the mix. During the summer, the regulations stated that an assistant should stand beside the mixing troughs with a fly-whisk to shoo away insects. So that differently priced cuts of meat did not get mixed up, butchers were required to offer them for sale clearly marked and separated. Fishmongers were instructed to carefully wash out their empty baskets and strew them with salt to prevent an unpleasant smell from transferring to subsequent batches of fish. Producers of ready-made foods had to abide by regulations concerning the ratio of the various ingredients. Even so, the eyes of the law could not be everywhere. And so there existed, conversely, books listing substitute products for expensive ingredients. They had titles such as 'Chemistry for the Cook' (*Kimiya li-l-Tabikh*). In this work, the renowned Arab philosopher al-Kindi (801–873) explained how to cook liver dishes containing no liver, or how to prepare sweetmeats without honey or sugar. Unfortunately, all that survives of this work of al-Kindi's is the title and a brief summary of its contents.

In the great cities of the Middle East the greatest quantity and variety of ready-made foods were to be found in the bazaars. In the countryside, where there are very few permanent markets to this day, the populace consisted in the main of people who catered for themselves and who could not have afforded the kinds of ready-made goods described in any case. Even in the Middle Ages, these cities had high population densities. Archaeological investigations of the medieval working-class districts of Cairo suggest that individual tenement blocks were built without any kitchens, since no evidence of fireplaces or provisions for extracting smoke have come to light. The people who inhabited these dwellings must have relied upon the cookshops for their sustenance. Similar conditions are thought to have prevailed in Istanbul during the Ottoman period.

Modern professional chefs

Indigenous sources about the kitchens of the Near and Middle East and their cuisines peter out in the 17th century. This may simply have been a result of the general cultural decline of the region at that time, or may point to a waning interest on the part of the literary elites for culinary matters. From the 19th century onwards, there are sporadic accounts of how to prepare certain meals or manufacture particular ingredients. These are the work of travellers and diplomats and are not especially enlightening. More detailed information is available from linguistic researchers and ethnologists, who since the late 19th century have been studying living conditions in Middle Eastern societies. The chief focus of attention for academics from the West has generally been the documentation of colloquial expressions and phrases, which they picked up from farmers, cooks and housewives. European ethnographers collected artefacts used in cooking, such as pots, crockery and utensils. European travellers, meanwhile, wrote accounts of the countries and peoples and their food and drink. Among the members of Western colonial administrations in North Africa, the Middle East and India there were at least a few enthusiasts with an interest in culinary matters, who related their experiences in the pages of colonial scientific journals. With the foreign seizure of political control from the mid-19th century onward and the associated cultural dominance of these regions by the colonial powers, the culinary practices in many countries started to change as the cuisine of the respective colonial powers began to take effect on the eating and drinking habits of the occupied countries. This first became apparent where the consumption of alcohol was concerned. In lands under French control, it was not long before the indigenous elite was slaking its thirst with imported cognac, while in British-run territories the preferred drink was whisky. Especially under the British, beer breweries were established in which master brewers from Germany, Czechoslovakia, Belgium and the Netherlands produced lagers and ales, albeit generally with a lower percentage of alcohol than the beers brewed in Europe.

In the hotel restaurants that mushroomed in all the major cities of the Middle East during this period, the emphasis until the 1950s was on offering exclusively European haute cuisine on the menu. Italian pasta dishes, but also French cuisine, were particularly popular. The wines to complement these dishes were imported. Only from the 1960s onwards did local wines acceptable to the European palate begin to be produced in such places as Lebanon, Egypt, Tunisia and Morocco. According to the principle of 'in for a penny, in for a pound', the wealthy native patrons of such establishments tended to go for higher-proof drinks like Remy Martin cognac, Scotch malt whiskies and German schnapps.

Yet it was not just the influence of colonial powers that has brought about changes in cooking and eating habits. The influx of labourers from South and Southeast Asia since the 1970s, particularly on the Arabian Peninsula, has prompted fears that the region's traditional indigenous cuisine might disappear. All of a sudden, Indian-, Filipino- or Vietnamese-inspired dishes began to infiltrate kitchens. In parallel with this trend, the number of Italian, Spanish, French, Vietnamese and Chinese restaurants in the major cities of the Middle East continued to grow apace. This development went so far that Arabic newspapers in the 1980s complained that there were only a handful of places left in the principal cities of Saudi Arabia where one could eat genuine

Arab food. In Saudi homes, meanwhile, Pakistani 'maids' were preparing the cuisine of their culture. But in those Middle Eastern countries that developed into tourist centres, European guests now also expected to encounter, alongside international cuisine, a home-grown cuisine of the kind they had become familiar with in certain restaurants in Europe. This expectation and the trend toward the re-nationalisation of food and cooking has increased since the 1990s, giving rise to a newly awakened interest in traditional cuisine, which went hand in hand with increased technical possibilities and an expansion in the choice of ingredients for sale.

The first effects of this rediscovery of Middle Eastern food were felt in up-market restaurants in the big cities. As early as the 1970s, it was possible to find in Beirut an outstanding Middle Eastern restaurant kitchen where Lebanese chefs re-imagined traditional recipes in a lighter and more elegant way. A decade later this renaissance had spread to all other states in the region.

Nowadays, in the large hotels belonging to international chains from Casablanca to Dubai, it is quite usual to find head chefs from the home country, as well as ones from European nations.

It is often the case that these Middle Eastern chefs (of both genders) have done their training in the restaurants in question, as well as working in the kitchens of internationally renowned chefs in Europe, America and Asia in order to gain experience and broaden their knowledge. Other chefs have begun their education in catering colleges where the primary focus is on the preparation of classic European haute cuisine dishes. One interesting factor is the uneven distribution of the sexes in professional kitchens. For instance, women are clearly in the majority in Moroccan hotel and restaurant kitchens. Connoisseurs of the Moroccan culinary scene claim that the first thing Moroccan diners do on booking a restaurant is to try and find out whether it has a female or a male head chef. If the latter, they opt for another establishment. In female-run kitchens, men perform tasks like washing-up or other ancillary duties.

In other regions, however, it is men who call the shots in professional kitchens. These chefs' knowledge often extends beyond a skill in preparing Middle Eastern dishes. They can be found nowadays as sous-chefs or chefs de partie in top Italian restaurants throughout Europe. It is noteworthy that cooks in high-profile hotel and restaurant kitchens in the Middle East have not only mastered the international repertoire but have also for some years now been striving to modernise the traditional recipes of their homelands. A prime example of one such modernised dish is the following, slightly modified, recipe devised by Abdel Hamid Badawy, head chef at the Marriott Hotel in the Cairo suburb of Zamalek. It is both simple and elegant.

Lentil soup with *fruits de mer*

Put 250 grams of yellow lentils, 1 coarsely chopped carrot and a small onion sliced into quarters into a large pan with 750 millilitres of good chicken stock and slowly bring to the boil. Turn down the heat and simmer for 20 minutes until the lentils are soft. Blend the soup until smooth in a mixer or with a hand blender and then stir in a handful of fresh basil and oregano leaves that you have cut roughly with scissors. Take the pan off the heat at this point. Peel some raw prawns and carefully de-vein them before frying gently in a skillet in a little olive oil and lemon juice, plus 3 finely chopped garlic cloves and a pinch of salt. Once the prawns have turned fully pink, remove and keep warm. In the same skillet, fry a handful of cubes of white bread on all sides to make croutons; at the end of cooking add two pressed garlic cloves and 1 tablespoon fresh dill to the pan. Season and flavour the lentil soup with salt, pepper and another sprinkle of chopped oregano. Divide the prawns up evenly between deep bowls before ladling over the soup and garnishing with the croutons.

Like other international celebrity chefs, these Middle Eastern chefs produce cookbooks, many of which are translated into various European languages. As in western European countries, they make cookery programmes for the numerous satellite-TV channels that exist in the region. Undoubtedly the most famous of these Middle Eastern chefs is the Lebanese Ramzi Choueiri (b. 1971), who not only runs a restaurant and writes cookbooks, but is known far beyond the borders of his small home country primarily thanks to his television show 'Chef Ramzi'. In this programme, he introduces his audience to traditional and modern Middle Eastern recipes while also offering handy hints about what kitchen implements, crockery and table decorations to use. His broadcasts are also available in the form of CDs.

Amateur cooks

Cooking as a leisure activity, as it has developed in Europe since the 1970s, was not at all widespread in the Middle Eastern world. Although people in the major conurbations would talk about high-end restaurants, amateur cookery has only really taken off since the start of the twenty-first century. The use of modern modes of communication is even more widespread in Middle Eastern societies than in some Western societies. Hobbyist chefs spend a great deal of time on social networking sites and blogs, comparing notes with like-minded people about various recipes and their practical execution. Contributors to these forums could scarcely be more diverse. Hobby cooks with large followings rub shoulders here with celebrities from all walks of life sharing stories of their home cookery exploits by way of trying to promote a particular image of themselves. For instance, Aisha, the daughter of the former Libyan president Muammar al-Gaddafi, liked to present herself as a gifted amateur cook. However, it was hard to determine the true state of play regarding her skill in the kitchen. In any event, these attempts to win popular credibility through culinary expertise (real or fabricated) does demonstrate the social significance attached to food and drink today. And the contrast to Western politicians and other prominent figures, who like to stress their preference for plain cooking, is clear and striking.

Cookbooks

Arab cuisine

Cookbooks represent some of the oldest written accounts in Arabic literature. Corresponding Persian and Turkish records only appear several centuries later. Thus, cookbooks dating from the period of Ottoman rule were initially for the most part translated from the Arabic to Turkish.

The first catalogue of available Arabic books in all manner of disciplines in an age when books still had to be produced by hand dates from the year 988. In this reference work, the author, Ibn al-Nadim (d. 995 or 998) also points to a number of cookbooks. Unfortunately, none of those he mentions have survived. We can therefore only surmise from the titles what their contents and recipes might have been. By contrast, some cookbooks from the Abbasid period have come down to us, despite the long timespan since their compilation. Medieval cookbooks from Syria, Egypt, North Africa and Moorish Spain (al-Andalus) can be found in the libraries of European, Near Eastern, Iranian and Indian ancient manuscript collections. Over the past thirty or forty years, several of these works have been rediscovered, published by knowledgeable philologists, and in some cases also translated into European languages. Two distinct types of work may be discerned among these ancient documents on the culture of cookery.

The first of these types conveys the impression that cooks are passing on recipes to other cooks, whereas the second type, despite containing numerous recipes, also has an entertainment function. It is characteristic of both traditional forms that the authors only very occasionally specify quantities of ingredients or cooking times. The writers must have proceeded from the assumption that their readership understood so much about cookery that they could safely dispense with such details. Far more so than is the case nowadays, the extent of a book was a cost issue. The scribes working on copying a manuscript would be paid according to its extent, with their remuneration being geared to the weight of the completed text folios. Generally speaking, all these cookbooks begin with a foreword in which the authors attempt to justify the content of the text. On the one hand they do this by pointing to passages from the Qur'an which stress the significance of food and drink as gifts from Allah. In passing they also emphasise how important it is to follow proper codes of practice in the kitchen so as to ensure that the dishes being prepared do not infringe the rules of ritual purity as laid down by Islamic law. Their forewords are also liberally sprinkled with quotations from Arabic wisdom literature.

Philosophical reflections and doctrines of traditional medicine were likewise woven in. It was not uncommon for the cookbook authors to also claim personal motives for writing their works and to maintain that they considered cooking a cultural achievement that warranted becoming the subject of a book.

Another feature that the two types of cookbook had in common was their description of the work involved in cooking and the personal requirements that the kitchen personnel needed to fulfil. These demands were not formulated very systematically, however. For example, one can encounter the following list of substantive requirements. A cook should be intelligent and familiar with the rules of the culinary art. He should have a feel for the art of cookery. A cook should ensure that his fingernails are always kept short, so that no dirt can accumulate beneath them. A cook should use stoneware or earthenware pots and only in exceptional circumstances ones made from tin-plated copper. For the kitchen fire, he should use wood, because it produces little smoke. He should be aware that rock-salt should always be used in cooking, and know how to prepare good stocks. The spices and herbs that were used in Arab cooking in the Middle Ages had to be thoroughly washed and very finely chopped or ground to a paste. Cooks were expected to take especially good care of their pots and pans. The cookbooks contain exhaustive instructions on how to clean them: they were first to be scoured with fine-ground brick dust before being rubbed over with dried potash and finally brushed clean with freshly picked lemon leaves. The books contain similar stipulations on the use of spices or methods of chopping or mincing fresh meat. At root, the purpose of these works was to set out the basic skills and knowledge that all cooks should have.

There was no uniformity in the way these different cookbooks organised their recipes. In each case, various categories of recipe are grouped together in separate chapters. However, the running order of these is very different between the books. All the same, a general tendency toward placing the sweets and desserts at the end of the books may be discerned. Some of the cookbooks begin by positing fundamental questions on the importance of food for people's general health.

Suitable meals were listed for the old and young, or for people with special health requirements like those who were convalescing, or who were physically infirm or pregnant, and the fundamental doctrines of medicine based on the 'four humours' were conveyed. The cookbooks were therefore related to the works of traditional Near Eastern medicine that deal with dietary matters and which had a major influence on European medicine. In their turn, certain works in Arabic on dietetics contain recipes that their physician authors considered beneficial to health. The prime objective of these guidelines on how to cook was therefore to attain a balanced form of food intake. Some of the cookbooks broached themes that had to do with the general business of running a household, such as tips on hygiene in the kitchen and even on flower-arranging or the use of incense in the home.

Alongside various recipes, the 'entertainment' type of cookbook also included anecdotes about particular personalities of the period and their experiences and preferences in the realm of food and drink. Chefs who were responsible for creating certain dishes were mentioned by name, and poems cited that were associated with particular dishes. Thus, Prince Ibrahim ibn al-Mahdi is said to have composed a poem on a kind of oven-baked dish by the name of *al-maghmūma* ('the covered one' – a reference to the bread covering the pot at the end of preparation). One stanza of this poem runs:

With herbs and vinegar artfully boil
Slices of meat in a pan in their own oil.
Top this with a layer of onions sweet,
Add eggplant and carrots and you're in for a treat!

Maghmūma (modern version)

This recipe was translated from the Arabic by David Waines and adapted for the modern kitchen by Ian Fraser.

Into a heavy casserole, place 675 grams of lamb shoulder, diced into small cubes, and 2 chopped chicken livers then cover with 175 grams of tinned chickpeas that have been liquidised to a paste. Coarsely chop 1 large onion and create a layer of the pieces on top of the meat and chickpeas. Over this sprinkle 2 teaspoons coriander seeds, lightly crushed, along with 10 stoned black olives cut in half and salt to taste. Cover the contents with water, mix thoroughly and simmer gently for an hour. Add more water if necessary. In the meantime, slice 1 large aubergine into rounds and spread with salt to leach out the bitter juices before rinsing off the excess salt, patting them dry with kitchen paper and frying them in olive oil until brown on both sides. At this stage blend 100 grams of crumbled sheep's or goat's cheese with 50 grams of ground walnuts and add to the casserole, mixing well. After allowing the aubergine slices to cool slightly also place them on top of the contents of the casserole and cook for another 10 minutes. Finally, tear 2 leftover flatbreads from the previous day into pieces and fry them in a pan in a little oil until crisp and brown, then arrange them evenly on a large plate and cover with the meat and vegetable mixture. Sprinkle with a little raspberry vinegar to finish. To serve, place an identical-sized plate on top and carefully invert so that the bread is now uppermost. If desired the *maghmūma* can be garnished with a few fresh asparagus spears that have been steamed or boiled in lightly salted water until tender.

A very special cookbook originated from North Africa in the late 13th century. All we know about its compiler, Ibn Razin al-Tujibi, is that he was born in the Andalusian city of Murcia. The title of the book instantly reveals its agenda: *Fadalat al-khiwan fi tayyibat al-ta'am wa'l-alwan* ('The Leftovers from the Table, with regard to all manner of delicacies'). In the introduction it becomes clear that the compiler had been forced to leave his homeland of Andalusia in the wake of the mounting success of the Christian attempt to reconquer Spain. In this book, al-Tujibi described and reconstructed the bill of fare that had been on offer on the Iberian Peninsula under Muslim rule. Yet in doing so, he did not confine himself to prestigious cuisine, as had been the case in all other

Arabic cookbooks of the medieval period, but also provided information on the simple dishes prepared in ordinary people's kitchen in al-Andalus.

Accordingly, al-Tujibi stands at the beginning of the tradition of a Muslim culture of memory, which reached its high point two centuries later and which endures to the present day. This commemorative culture aimed to vividly recall all aspects of life in Moorish Andalusia. One such area was the region's cuisine. In modern cookbooks and articles on the cultural history of food, Moroccan authors in particular like to point to the connection that can be reconstructed between modern North African cookery and the cuisine of medieval Andalusia as documented by al-Tujibi.

Ottoman cuisine

To date, only a handful of original cookbooks on the cuisine of the Ottoman Empire have come to light. Most of what we know derives from economic historians who have studied the household expenditures of various social groups and different periods. From this material, it is possible to gain a good overview of the products that were available to the cooks from the various social classes. One rich source is afforded by works that may be broadly categorised as guides to correct behaviour. These works come primarily from the 16th century and later. They often appear under the umbrella title of *Menafiü l-nas* ('Practical Guidelines for People'). The most important topic covered was how to conduct oneself when invited out to eat. One of the most well-known works of this kind was compiled by Nidai Mehmet Efendi. His text contains instructions on how to prepare no fewer than 88 recipes from Ottoman cuisine, as well as numerous other recipes for meals and beverages. It is impossible to know how many more Ottoman cookbooks may be languishing in the form of manuscripts in the numerous libraries of Turkey, just waiting to be discovered.

Persian cuisine

Persian cookbooks only began to be written during the reign of the Safavids (i.e. from 1501 onwards). Thus far, only a handful have been discovered and edited. They too were written by cooks for cooks who were working at the royal court or for the country's foremost elite.

Some of the recipes described in these works must surely go back to the reign of the preceding dynasty, the Timurids (ruled 1370 – 1501/7), a clear indication of the Central Asian influence on Persian cuisine. At the heart of these recipes, and hence no doubt of Persian haute cuisine in general from the 16th century onwards, are numerous instructions on the different ways of preparing rice. In addition, even in recipe books from that period, there are recipes in which meat and fruit – or fruit derivatives like juice or syrup – are combined. The strongly regional nature of the modern Iranian culinary tradition cannot be found in the ancient cookbooks. One exception to this general rule, however, is the famous dish known as *fesenjān*, which reappears time and again down the ages.

Khoresh fesenjān (modern version)

Grind 250 grams of shelled walnut halves in a blender until fine. Coarsely chop 1 large onion and sweat gently on the hob in olive oil in a casserole until translucent; sprinkle on a good knife-tip's worth of ground turmeric and stir. Now add the walnuts to the onions and fry for another 5 mins until the mix is lightly browned. Add 500 millilitres of cold water, bring to the boil and leave to simmer on the lowest heat possible for at least three hours, stirring every now and then to stop it sticking. If the sauce becomes too firm, add a splash of cold water to loosen. Meanwhile, in a separate pan quickly sear duck or chicken meat, skinned and boned and add to it another large onion, finely chopped. Season with a little more ground turmeric. Using a pestle and mortar, crush a few saffron threads and put them into the meat mix with a little warm water. Deglaze the meat pan with boiling water and braise over a low heat for 1 hour. Finally add another splash of warm water and let this bubble briefly before removing from the heat. Now add a 5 millilitre spoonful of pomegranate molasses to the walnut sauce, stir it in and bring the mix back to a gentle simmer. After a few minutes, combine the braised duck or chicken pieces with their juices to the walnut sauce and cook the whole dish for a further hour. Serve with plenty of plain boiled white long-grain (basmati) rice.

Mughal cuisine

The respective compilers of medieval Persian and Indian cookbooks are at pains to stress, time and again, that the other's cuisine was influenced by their own. What is certainly true is that there are many linguistic similarities between the two cultures in their culinary terminology, and that close cultural ties had always existed between Iran and India. Yet at the same time there were also definite divergences between the two cuisines which clearly manifested themselves in cooking techniques. The oldest Indo-Muslim cookbook to have survived is also the first to appear in the Indian Muslim language of Urdu. The book in question is the *Ni'matnāma* ('Book of Pleasures') by Sultan Giyath Shahi of Mandu (r. 1456–1500). This book is distinct from all other oriental cookbooks of the Middle Ages in having numerous miniatures that illustrate the recipes. Always depicted in the centre of these is the Sultan, recognisable by his extravagant moustache. On some of the miniatures, he is clearly giving the chefs instructions on how to prepare certain dishes. Furthermore, these illustrations provide something of an overview of the kitchen equipment and cooking techniques that were used at the time. On the other hand, the book lacks a general introduction. It launches straight into the recipes, which give the impression of having been prepared by the Sultan himself. Several of the recipes begin with the phrase: 'A better way to prepare this dish is...' Alongside numerous rice and samosa recipes, various ways of serving betel nuts are noted, together with hints on how to make perfumes and incense. The book also contains certain recipes involving medical hints on the best food to feed to invalids suffering from stomach problems or eye defects. Because brightly shining eyes were an integral part of the oriental ideal of beauty, any tips on maintaining and enhancing this quality were most welcome, as was a list of ingredients for creating aphrodisiacs or, more prosaically, for medicaments to reduce a fever (antipyretics).

Sultan's Giyath Shahi's recipe for samosas

Samosas are small savoury pastries filled with a meat or vegetable mix and deep-fried in oil. Traditionally, the pastry was made with flour, yeast, ghee (clarified butter), water and salt.

This is Giyath Shahi's alternative version of samosa: Take a quantity of finely minced venison and a portion of ghee flavoured with fennel. After mixing the minced meat with some strands of saffron, put it in the hot ghee. Dry-roast together small amounts of sea salt and cumin and then add this to the meat, with pinches of cloves, coriander seed and a quarter rati [a tiny amount] of musk, and fry until thoroughly cooked through. Now add half a finely chopped onion and roughly half that quantity of finely minced root ginger to the meat mix. When everything is well cooked, sprinkle rosewater on the dish. Remove from the heat and allow to cool slightly before making up the samosas, folding the pastry over until it forms a well-sealed triangular parcel. Carefully skewer each samosa on a stick, fry them in sweet-tasting ghee until golden-brown and serve them when they have cooled slightly and the pastry has softened. This same method can be used for any type of meat you prefer to use as a filling.

The second cookbook of medieval Indo-Muslim cuisine that has been preserved goes by the name of Nushka-e-Shajehani (Shah Jahan's Copy'). Shah Jahan (1592–1666) was the fifth ruler of the Mughal dynasty. His book contains a large number of *pulao*s (rice dishes), which are combined with various types of meat. Among the recipes for the preparation of meat there are some involving beef, which is highly unusual in India not just in modern times but also for cuisine during the Mughal period, indeed as unfamiliar as recipes in which cow's milk is an ingredient. The total disregard for his Hindu subjects, for which Shah Jahan was notorious, thus even found expression in his rules for the kitchen.

Modern cookbooks

Although, generally speaking, it was men who monopolised the role of chef in the Middle Ages – at royal courts and in the households of the upper echelons of society, in any event – Egyptian women chefs at least had a good reputation, with their skills securing them employment as far afield as Syria. In more humble households with their own kitchens, the responsibility for preparing food lay with the women of the house. Mothers handed down the requisite knowledge to their daughters. Especially from the mid-20th century on, this tradition began to change more or less rapidly in all the different nation-states of the Middle East. After it became compulsory for girls to attend school in many regions, fewer and fewer women were educated in kitchencraft, especially in the urban households of the middle and upper classes. Little by little, young women started to engage in paid employment outside the home. In the wake of this development, the growth of small family units meant that many young women received only the most rudimentary of instruction from their mothers in how to prepare all kinds of dishes. As a result, cookery schools were established, for example in Baghdad in the 1950s, where young upper-middle class women learned culinary skills. An intended side-benefit of this training was also that they would be in a position to efficiently manage their kitchen staff.

However, a study of the newspapers of the period reveals yet another major social change. Time and again during the 1960s, the same complaint is heard in cities the length and breadth of the Near and Middle East, from Casablanca to Karachi, namely that young women with only a very tenuous grasp of cookery were increasingly falling back on tinned provisions and later on deep-frozen food, claimed to be more expensive and less healthy than freshly prepared meals. The only alternative at their disposal was the even more expensive restaurants. This trend led in a country like Lebanon, for example, to modern cookery books making their first appearance on the shelves of bookstores as early as the 1950s. Frequently, these offered an extraordinary mix of Arab and Western, but above all French and Italian cuisine.

During the 1960s, the growing influence of pan-Arab nationalism saw a resurgence of cookbooks specifically on Arab cuisine. These texts were very much in step with the ideological notion of a single Arab nation, an aspiration that would also be realised in the kitchen. While the many books that have been published since the 1980s still talk in general terms about an Arab cuisine, many of the actual recipes expressly point to a specific regional provenance. The rise of regional consciousness within the Arab world also witnessed a shift in the content of cookbooks. Thus, a cookbook appeared in 1985 in Kuwait containing specifically Kuwaiti recipes. Prior to this, there had been a succession of political clashes between the states of Iraq and Kuwait, with Iraq claiming sovereignty over the smaller, oil-rich sheikhdom on the Persian Gulf. The cookbook, which was presented to all visitors to Kuwaiti embassies throughout the world, was a subtle attempt on the part of the authorities in Kuwait to underscore the country's national identity. Yet almost simultaneously, an Iraqi cookbook on the cuisine of Baghdad also appeared. The differences between the recipes in the two books do not strike a reader as very significant.

Subsequently more and more Arab cookbooks with regional or rather national titles have been published. Some use the Arabic word *fann* ('art') in their title. The most remarkable of these publications hails from Saudi Arabia. Social change in the kingdom over a long period had meant that modern Saudi families only rarely ate the dishes that had once been commonplace among their parents and grandparents. Moreover, many of the cooking staff came from outside the country and were preparing the cuisine of their home countries. It was no longer at all common to find restaurants with Saudi or Arab cuisine in the large cities. Instead, there were any number of Italian, French or Asian – predominantly Indian, Chinese and Japanese eating opportunities. A group of Saudi women cultural historians and social scientists regarded this trend as potentially undermining the national identity of the country. With the support of a Saudi princess these experts now began, in a systematic survey of older women, to collect and preserve for posterity the various methods of preparing several hundred traditional regional dishes. Professional cooks developed this data into recipes that could be made in modern kitchens. The resulting book was a runaway success and was reprinted several times over. Whether it succeeded in changing day-to-day cooking practices is doubtful, though. But at least the whole enterprise served to stimulate general public interest in Saudi Arabia in its own culinary traditions, as well as having a knock-on effect on neighbouring states.

Modern cookbooks had existed in Iran since the late 19th century. These early examples still adhered closely to the original type of literary cookbook with recipes from the French culinary tradition, supplemented with anecdotes or poems. Alongside some standard and certain more showy recipes from the canon of Persian cuisine, the first cookbooks of the 1920s, which were obviously aimed at the 'modern' Tehran housewife, also included chapters with recipes from the French culinary tradition. Over the course of the decades, this section on French cuisine kept expanding. The main purpose of such books was evidently to acquaint their female readers with modern methods of housekeeping. In the process they helped foster an extraordinary conception of modernity and the West among the Iranian middle classes. An empirically based investigation would have shown that although modern appliances were being used in these households, people still continued to turn out traditional Persian cuisine. In other words, the French recipes in the cookery books had another function entirely. As the Austrian Iranologist, Bert G. Fragner, has indicated, they represented a document of exoticism to their readership, who could swap notes on visits to afternoon tea with their circle of friends about the peculiarities of this distant cuisine. The cookbooks that were produced in Iran after the Islamic Revolution of 1979 differ from preceding ones through the complete absence of alcohol in them; the number of Western recipes was also reduced. Anyone in the West who is interested in the cuisine of modern Iran can consult a number of 'ethnographic cookbooks' (Fragner) now on the market.

These are often written by émigré Iranians who are concerned to save traditional dishes from oblivion and who have a mission to introduce the huge diversity and quality of Persian cuisine to a receptive Western audience.

The first printed Turkish cookbook dates back to the Ottoman period. The work first appeared in 1844 in Ottoman Turkish under the title *Melce üt-tabbahīn* ('The Refuge of Cooks'), and remained constantly in print right up to 1889. Its principal contents were recipes from the Topkapi Palace. If one compares the recipes in this book with the Ottoman records on kitchen expenditure in the Sultan's palace, there is a clear concordance with the ingredients mentioned there. Among other things, one of the most remarkable features of this work are recipes that are quite clearly French in origin. These were used almost exclusively in preparing dishes for Europeans who were on official state visits.

From around 1900, a whole series of women's magazines began to appear in the Ottoman Empire. Alongside topics like fashion, literature and other fine arts subjects, questions on running a household and child-rearing, these publications also regularly included recipes. In 1924 and 1926, two further cookbooks were published, one of which dealt solely with the preparation of desserts in the palace kitchen. In the wake of the enormous political upheavals brought about by Kemal Atatürk's reforms, which were enacted in the Turkish Republic after the collapse of the Ottoman Empire in 1918, interest in Ottoman cuisine declined sharply. The recipes were too expensive and elaborate, while domestic kitchens in the burgeoning cities were too small. A few 'republican' cookbooks were produced that were more suited to the new social circumstances. But whether out of criticism of the former monarchist regime or sheer curiosity about recipes from the 'West', a noticeable trend in Turkish cookbooks right up to the 1960s was a pronounced distancing from Ottoman cuisine, the focus turning instead to promoting Anatolian peasant cookery. This tendency was reinforced by Turkish ethnographers' mounting interest in the diverse forms of traditional cuisine that existed in the various regions of Turkey.

Granted, to begin with, their activities were of a predominantly academic nature. Only in the 1980s was there a resurgence of interest in Turkish culinary traditions and Ottoman cuisine. What prompted this was the growth in tourism and foreign guests' requests for typical Turkish dishes. Accordingly, it was the Turkish tourist board that seized the initiative; at conferences on Turkish cuisine, ideas were mooted on how to reconstruct and more assiduously promote a sophisticated indigenous cuisine. Plans were also made to establish a Museum of Turkish Cuisine. The brother and sister Feyzi and Nevin Halici became the driving force behind making these schemes a reality. Through numerous academic treatises and cookbooks, they helped to constantly raise awareness of Turkish cuisine, initially in the hotel trade and gastronomic circles, but thereafter in ordinary Turkish households as well.

As happened in many other countries, first and foremost the Western world, the period since the 1990s has also witnessed an explosion in the number of cookbooks published in Turkey. These titles cover both a national cuisine as well as different regional cuisines. Ottoman cookery has been made accessible to the modern housewife, and even the cookery of the masters of the mystical strain of Islam known as Sufism has been documented. Even so, sceptical observers have doubted whether this renewed interest in cookbooks will actually have a lasting effect on cooking habits

– either in the majority of restaurants in Turkey or in private households. The perfectly acceptable fare produced in people's homes in Turkey might be termed 'Mainstream' Turkish cuisine. However, the high degree of refinement that characterised cooking in the 19th century has been lost. In its place, a number of commonplace Arab appetisers have found their way onto the Turkish menu, for instance *hummus* (chickpea and tahini purée). At the time of writing, it is clear that if the Turkish culinary culture is to progress, it will be up to high-end restaurants in Istanbul and other tourist centres to make the running.

The ongoing political conflicts both between and within the various states of the region make any analysis of the modern cookbooks among the Muslim population of the Indian Subcontinent a highly complicated undertaking.

There is a wide range of cookbooks which propagate the idea of something called 'Indian' cuisine. Many of them quite unequivocally hark back to the history and the recipes of the Mughal period. In stark contrast to these, there exists a large body of cookbooks whose emphasis is on the many regional cuisines of the Subcontinent. They include works relating to the regions in the north of India that are home to large Muslim minority populations. It is notable that these regional cookbooks make frequent reference to the cuisine of the Raj, the period of British colonial rule from 1858 to 1947.

In the present day, the cookbooks and videos produced by the chef Zubeida Tariq enjoy great popularity; although she was born in Hyderabad, India, her recipes have a large following throughout both India and Pakistan. In fact, she now lives in Karachi in Pakistan. Her books are presented in a very simple way and are at the same time decidedly practical. Meanwhile her videos remain rooted in a very traditional format. In contrast to those produced by Arab celebrity chefs, who usually appear as soloists, Zubeida Tariq always has a young woman by her side playing the part of the inquisitive pupil. Despite having some similarities with the general run of Indian cuisine, her recipes are noticeably aimed at a Muslim public, given that some of her dishes call for the use of veal or beef. Needless to say, there are no recipes involving pork. Indeed, while pork is not a very common ingredient in Indian cookery at all, it is not wholly unknown in the cuisine of Southern India. It is striking that Zubeida Tariq's cookbooks contain chapters relating to special occasions like children's birthday parties or the major religious festivals, and also stray extensively into the realms of Chinese cuisine. By contrast, cookbooks that endeavour to do nothing but reconstruct Mughal cuisine have hitherto been published in Great Britain for the most part.

All in all, in presenting an overview of modern cookbooks from around the Near and Middle East and India it becomes clear that more commonalities than differences can be identified. They have all been shaped in some way by the conventions of modern cookbook production in the West and have taken on board many aspects of their design, with professional food styling and photography and line drawings of the different stages of preparation. The same goes for the way the contents are organised into appetisers, fish, meat main courses and desserts. To date no extensive lifestyle coffee-table books including recipes have appeared on the market in these regions, however. It will surely only be a matter of time before they do.

Since the early 1980s, it has also been possible to find the occasional work on the health aspects of food and drink in the bookstores of Middle Eastern cities. Some have been written by medics, while others are the work of Muslim religious scholars. Generally speaking these are small-format volumes which seldom run to more than a hundred pages or so. Many of these books refer to the 'prophetic medicine' (*al-tibb al nabawi*), namely the collection and interpretation of sayings by the Prophet Muhammad on healthy living. Muslim authors of modern works on a healthy diet invoke the 'prophetic medicine' in the hope that this will lend their own texts greater authority in the eyes of devout followers of Islam. Television programmes and DVDs on this subject have also since appeared. In addition, small-format booklets with titles like 'Appetising Dishes' have short introductory essays treating the healthy aspects of cooking and stressing the need to pay attention to the quality of meat and vegetables when doing the shopping. The process of washing food, primarily vegetables, is described as painstaking detail. On the other hand, virtually nothing is said about how to handle and prepare other ingredients such as meat and fish. Even in newspapers in the various regions of the Near and Middle East it has since become customary for regular columns or even whole pages to be devoted to health and a balanced diet.

Itinerant Ingredients – The Flow of Commodities to and from the East

Even in the pre-Islamic period, various types of grain, vegetables and fruits had already been brought to the Near and Middle East from India, the islands comprising what is now Indonesia and from China. The later systematic improvement of transport and trade routes leading into the Islamic heartland, above all during the reign of the Abbasids, brought about a significant increase in the import of agricultural crops. Many new crops appeared in markets in areas that were under Abbasid control. From there they were taken to the Muslim-run regions of North Africa, Sicily and the Iberian Peninsula, even reaching as far as the Islamic states south of the Sahara in West Africa and the East African coast. It has even been shown that imports from the Islamic world, particularly from Sicily and the Iberian Peninsula, also reached the Balkan region via the moribund but still extant Byzantine Empire. And it was along such routes that they finally reached the mercantile centres of Western and Central Europe. We owe our knowledge of the network of trade routes from India and Southeast Asia primarily to the accounts written by Arab geographers and universal historians of the period. These reports have been substantiated by archaeological discoveries which have yielded important information about the spread of the different crops.

From the Far East and the West to the Islamic world

Grains

In both the classical and modern cookbooks hailing from regions of the Far East, three staple crops stand out: wheat, millet and rice. Millet and common wheat (*Triticum aestivum*), which were almost certainly first known in areas of what is now Afghanistan, had been cultivated in the Near and Middle East since time immemorial. Durum wheat (*Triticum durum*) and rice (*Oryza sativa*), on the other hand, are grain varieties that first had to be imported to the region. The systematic cultivation of rice was conducted on a large scale in India, Burma, Thailand and China. From there, it was taken to the Philippines and to the Southeast Asian island world of modern Indonesia. According to the ancient geographer Strabo, rice was already a familiar crop in Iran, Mesopotamia and the Jordan Valley by the 2nd century BC. It is also reputed to have been imported in small quantities for medicinal purposes to the pre-Islamic Arabian Peninsula and East Africa, but not to have been cultivated there. Under Islamic rule, rice cultivation became widely established in all places where there was sufficient availability of fresh water, which is essential for rice crops to grow and flourish. From this period onwards, rice production was intensified in the easternmost parts of the Islamic heartland such as Iran and Mesopotamia.

Farmers began to cultivate rice in the region around the rivers Tigris and Euphrates, where a complex systems of irrigation canals was built, as well as along the southern shores of the Caspian Sea. Other cultivation areas arose subsequently around the city of Herat in the west of present-day Afghanistan, in the province of Sind in modern Pakistan and even in the Ferghana Valley in Central Asia. The harvests from the Jordan Valley supplied the whole of Palestine with rice. It was also said to have been grown in Yemen. There were rice paddies along the Nile and in the Faiyum Oasis, where it is no longer cultivated. In North Africa however, aside from a few sites in the south of Morocco, rice growing was not possible due to the lack of water. By contrast, in Muslim-controlled Sicily, large acreages of paddy fields were established. Above all rice cultivation became widespread in Spain following the Muslim conquest. The historical sources tell of a region around Valencia that was the centre of Iberian rice production. Surprisingly, one even reads of rice being cultivated on the Balearic island of Majorca. Furthermore, the Arabs took rice cultivation to the most far-flung outposts of the Islamic world, like the Volga River valley in the north and East Africa in the south. By the 14th century rice had formed the staple diet of the population of Mogadishu in Somalia.

Its broad distribution across this region is believed to have begun as early as the 10th century. It may even be the case that the first forms of rice production date back to the pre-Islamic period. Besides, an African variety of rice (*Oryza glaberrima*) is reputed to have been in existence long before Arabs first appeared in West Africa. Yet nor can the possibility be excluded that it was the

Arabs who introduced Asiatic strains of rice into this region. Both Arab and European travellers reported that the rice on offer in West Africa was of just as high a quality as the rice they were familiar with in their homelands.

In the Ottoman Empire in the 16th century, rice was still not an everyday staple food, though it had already been planted in a few regions of the vast empire. Areas of rice cultivation were located in Rumelia, in Anatolia near the city of Sinope and around the shores of the Black Sea. By the second half of that century, however, it had already begun to appear on the bill of fare served in dervish monasteries. For instance, there is a report from Diyarbakir in this period that visitors to the dervish monastery there were being served a rice dish with melons that was spiced with cloves and cinnamon. Nonetheless the product remained somewhat exotic, which must have had an impact on its price. For its principal function continued to be as an additive to soups. A rice soup of this type was renowned for being especially fortifying and was fed to invalids and convalescents. Sometime after 1670, it is widely assumed that rice supplanted wheat bread as the most commonplace staple food in Turkey.

Sharab al-rumman (pink rice)
literally 'Pomegranate drink'

Peel and finely chop 6 medium onions and sweat them lightly in oil. Pour 100 millilitres of pomegranate juice with a pinch of salt and 200 millilitres of cold water over the onions and bring to the boil. Add 2 cups well-washed long-grain (basmati) rice and 1 cup shelled walnuts to the mix and simmer gently for 20 minutes until the rice is cooked through.

Durum wheat, which in the modern kitchen is especially beloved by fans of pasta, is a relatively new cereal crop. Food historians are of the opinion that it originated in Ethiopia or the Eastern Mediterranean (Levant) as the result of a mutation of the primitive wheat form emmer (*Triticum dicoccum*) and moreover at a relatively late stage; certainly, durum wheat was unknown in Classical Antiquity. The wheat that was shipped in large quantities to Rome was emmer. Even works on agriculture from the Hellenistic period make no mention of durum wheat. The first signs of its cultivation emerge from archaeological evidence, which points to its presence in Egypt immediately prior to the Islamic conquest of the country in 642. Yet thereafter it was the Arabs who were responsible for spreading this crop to all the regions that they either overran during their campaigns of military subjugation or with which they traded through their extensive mercantile network. Even so, the Arabic language has no special term for durum wheat; the word *hinta* simply means 'wheat' without any differentiation. One possible exception, though, may be the word *burr*, which was used in medieval Yemen and also denotes wheat. But Arab authors point to differences between this grain and *hinta* that strongly suggest it may have been durum. However, the term *burr* did not become established as the standard word for durum wheat. Even Arab historiographers, geographers and travellers note that it was especially highly prized in those areas of the Near and Middle East characterised by low levels of rainfall, because it was well suited to arid soils. Special local forms of durum wheat evolved in Spain, North Africa, Central Asia and Ethiopia. Another advantage of durum wheat proved to be its long storage life. The geographer al-ʿUmari (1300–1384) reported that stocks of this variety of wheat were stored in grain silos in North Africa for eighty years, and that this long period in storage had even served to enhance its purity and quality. Meanwhile, the Algerian historiographer al-Maqqari (d. 1632) – who dedicated his principal work entitled *The Breath of Perfume from the Branch of Green Andalusia* to Moorish Spain (al-Andalus), since been lost by the Muslims to Christian reconquest – even went so far as to claim that the (durum) wheat in Zaragoza could stay fresh for a hundred years. The growing popularity of durum wheat as an important staple cereal crop is also attested by the development of new recipes utilising it from the 12th and 13th centuries onward.

By that time, people had worked out that the high gluten content of durum wheat made it ideal for the manufacture of semolina. This discovery gave rise to the well-known North African dish couscous, which can form the basis of both savouries and sweets. By the 13th century, couscous was a familiar sight not only in Morocco, Algeria and Tunisia, but also in Spain and Egypt, and even as far afield as Mesopotamia.

Couscous with chicken

This recipe comes from Taroudant. There are as many couscous recipes as there are Moroccan housewives and professional cooks of both genders.

In a large pan or tagine, fry 1 kilogram chicken pieces (bone-in) in olive oil, then add to this 2 thinly sliced onions, 3 finely chopped cloves of garlic, a small tin of tomatoes, 2 washed red peppers cut into broad strips, a handful of leaf coriander and double that quantity of flat-leafed parsley – both very finely chopped – 2 tablespoons finely chopped fresh root ginger, an inch of ground cloves, ground cinnamon, grated nutmeg, turmeric powder, 10 saffron threads steeped in a little warm water, and finally 1 litre of hot water. Simmer for 45 minutes until the meat is tender. With a slotted spoon, remove the meat and the red pepper strips from the tagine and keep them warm. Continue to simmer and reduce the remaining liquid. Meanwhile, soften 150 grams of raisins in some warm water, dry-roast 50 grams of pine kernels and keep these both warm as well. Prepare 1 packet couscous (500 grams) according to the instructions on the box or bag, then in a large bowl heap the finished couscous into a neat pile, garnish with the pine nuts and raisins and surround it with the meat and paprika mix. Serve the broth separately in a jug, and pass round a bowl of spicy harissa paste (preferably homemade) so that people can help themselves if desired.

Another way of using durum wheat is to make noodles from it. The Arabic word for noodles is *itriyya*. The term only began to appear in Arabic dictionaries in the 14th century, although it was already to be found in cookbooks and medical works in Arabic in the preceding century. We may safely assume that these noodles were made from durum wheat. Some form of noodles are thought to have been in use in Arab kitchens from as early as the 9th century, though it is impossible to say with any certainty whether these were made from durum wheat.

There has been much speculation about the origins of noodles. The old legend that it was Marco Polo who brought this method of using grain back to Europe has now been thoroughly debunked. There is also general agreement among scholars that the ancient classical world did not know about noodles. However, it is hard to determine exactly when noodles did finally fetch up in the cooking pots of the Near and Middle East. According to medieval Arabic cookbooks, there were two distinct types of noodle. On the one hand, long, thin, spaghetti-like noodles were referred to in cookbooks from Baghdad and Damascus, but also in Iran, as *rishta*. This same sort were called *itriyya* in Andalusian and North African cookbooks. The Catalan word for noodles, *aletria*, derives from this. In the northern Italian region of Liguria, they are known simply as *tria*. The second type comprises shorter, extremely thin noodles, which in the east of the Arabic-speaking world were given the name *sha'riyya*, from the Arabic word *sha'r* for hair. In the western Arabic region they are called *fidaush*, the root of the Spanish word *fideos* and the Italin *fedelini*. The German cultural historian Peter Peter informs us that noodle makers in Genoa in 1574 referred to themselves as *fidelari*. Long before that, the Arab geographer al-Idrisi (1099–1161), in his work *Nuzhat al-mushtaq* ('The Book of Pleasant Journeys into Faraway Lands'), which he devoted to King Roger II of Sicily (1095–1154), had written: 'To the west of Termini there is a place by the name of Trabia. It is an enchanting place whereat to stop a while, with its constantly flowing water and many mills. There is a broad plain there with extensive estates, where they produce large amounts of *ytria* (from the Arabic *itriyya*) and export it far and wide.'

This adoption of Arabic words to denote various sorts of noodles certainly does hint at a direct Arabic provenance for this Italian staple foodstuff. Yet only few recipes for how to make or use noodles can be found in medieval Arabic cookbooks. Instead, they tend to appear mostly in the context of comparisons: for example, one recipe instructs the user to slice courgettes 'as finely as *rishta*'. In modern Near and Middle Eastern cookbooks, the talk is chiefly of vermicelli; combinations of noodles and rice are especially popular in this region.

Sugar cane

Little is known about the origins of sugar cane cultivation, though it is thought to have begun in the early civilisations of India or in China. From there the crop made its way very slowly westward. In the 7th century, sugar canes were being grown in Iran and sugar produced from the raw material. But until the start of the Islamic calendar – i.e. AD 622 – sugar canes did not advance any further west than this. Under Muslim rule, cultivation of this crop first continued to expand within Iran but also spread to Mesopotamia. The existing sources do not describe in detail how this expansion proceeded, but from the 10th century onward a far-reaching distribution of sugar cane cultivation can be traced from the works of Arab geographers. Alongside Mesopotamia, the principal regions of cultivation in Iran have been identified as the coast of the Persian Gulf, in the province of Kerman and along the Strait of Hormuz, in Gorgan and on the shores of the Caspian Sea. In addition, there was also a cluster of plantations further to the east, in the Sind province of India. In the 10th century, some individual details emerge about cane sugar production in the Near and Middle East, with accounts of sugar cane cultivation in Ghouta (the oasis outside Damascus) and in the Jordan Valley as far north as Jericho. The crop was also grown along the Mediterranean coast of the Levant, from Tripoli to Sidon and Tyre and down to Acre. From there, sugar cane plants were transported to the islands of the Eastern Mediterranean. In contrast, sugar cane had been cultivated in Egypt from as early as the 8th century.

The main focuses of cultivation were in the Nile Delta, in the Fayyum Oasis and in certain regions of Upper Egypt. Arab geographers and travellers from various countries speak of the superabundance of sugar in Egypt. There is firm evidence that sugar canes were grown in North Africa, Sicily and Spain. Centres of cultivation lay in the south of what is today Tunisia, Algiers, the Sous region of Morocco and in Marrakesh. Sugar grown in Sous, which was produced in great quantities, was reputed to be of very high quality. In Spain the cane sugar production centres lay along the Guadalquivir River near Seville, on the southern coast of Andalucía near Malaga or further inland around Granada, and even as far north as Castellón. Agricultural instruction books, such as that written by Ibn al-'Awwam (late 12th century), reveal some of the details of how the crop was grown. In the south, sugar cane had reached Yemen and Ethiopia by the 8th century at the latest, and may even have already existed there in pre-Islamic times. It may also have been brought to Oman in the pre-Islamic period. In view of the good trade links that Oman fostered with the islands off the coast of East Africa, it comes as no surprise to read reports of the high-quality sugar being produced in Zanzibar in the 10th century. From there, the crop was exported south to Madagascar. Even so, sugar continued to be the less favoured method of sweetening food. Medieval cookbooks universally prefer honey, which was more expensive and so had a higher status in the kitchen.

Like the word 'candy' (from *qand*, 'cane sugar'), even the word 'sugar' comes from Arabic. Europeans first became acquainted with this sweetening agent from the East on the Iberian Peninsula, and through encountering it on the Crusades to the Middle East. Like rice, sugar too was first prized as a remedy, to which invigorating properties were attributed. In Arab pharmacy, sugar was a frequent constituent element of medicines that were composed of a number of active ingredients. In Europe this combination was used by way of preserving the other ingredients, through increasing the proportion of sugar in the mix so as to be able to produce medicines and store them for later use. Accordingly, they were often manufactured in the form of lozenges. These in turn were much favoured as aids to digestion after sumptuous meals.

Yet sugar was also known as a pure luxury product; its first use in medieval Europe was for lavish sugarwork table decorations displayed at important social banquets hosted by rulers or the senior clergy. The sugar was crafted into sculptures that were then eaten by the assembled company at the end of the meal. Right up to the late 18th century, sugar remained a scarcely unaffordable indulgence for the great majority of the population. It was only the discovery that sugar could be processed from sugar beet that turned it into a cheap mass-market product.

Candied rose petals

Candied rose petals can be purchased in specialist shops or confectioners, but are also quite straightforward to make at home.

Take 50 grams red rose petals from blooms that have not been sprayed with any insecticides and carefully wipe them with a clean cloth or a piece of kitchen paper. Use kitchen scissors to snip away the white parts where the stems begin. Beat 3 egg whites to form soft, but not stiff, peaks. Shake a generous layer of sugar onto a marble board. Dip the rose petals in the egg white to coat both sides, press them onto the sugar layer and sprinkle the upper surface with more sugar. Leave to dry in a warm place or a barely warmed oven for 12 hours. Finally arrange them carefully in layers in a wide, flat porcelain or plastic container. The rose petals grow harder and more brittle the longer they are stored, but still remain perfectly usable.

Citrus fruits

Certain citrus fruits have enjoyed great popularity, not just in the Middle East. Bitter (Seville) oranges were known in the Abbasid Empire from as early as the beginning of the 10th century. Ibn Wahshiyya (9th/10th centuries), who was renowned for his work *Nabataean Agriculture*, wrote at length about their cultivation. Oranges were likewise cultivated in Andalusia in the 10th century, as shown by the *Patio de las Naranjos* in Córdoba. To begin with, oranges may well have been used as ornamental shrubs. Later it was primarily Seville oranges that were planted as commercial fruit trees in the area between Mesopotamia and North Africa and in Sicily but also in Yemen. In the 15th and 16th centuries they also found their way to Sub-Saharan Africa.

Limes, from India, were also known to Arab authors from the early 10th century. We know for sure that they spread throughout the Islamic world between the 10th and 12th centuries, except for perhaps to areas south of the Sahara.

Their juice or skins were used for perfumes or for flavouring dishes. Yet is it above all lemons that one thinks of nowadays as an essential ingredient in Middle Eastern cookery. A typical ingredient in North African cuisine, for example, is preserved lemon.

Preserved lemons

Rinse out a glass preserving jar with a tight-fitting lid in boiling water. According to the size of your jar, wash and scrub 4 to 6 unwaxed organic lemons under hot, running water and then cut into quarters, but not right through so that the pieces remain attached at the stem end. Open up the cut lemons, stuff them with as much salt as you can and put them into the jar, pressing them down so that they are squashed together. Leave for 3–4 days, after which timer the lemons will have released some of their juice. Press down firmly once more and top up the jar with some more freshly squeezed lemon juice. Leave the jar in a cool place for 8 weeks, occasionally opening to make sure that the pieces are well submerged in the lemony brine. The lemons should ideally be completely immersed in the liquid. When the skins have fully softened, the lemons can be extracted and used one by one. Scrape away the pulp from each segment and discard; only the skin is used, cut into thin strips or tiny pieces for adding to tagines and other dishes. Rinse each piece of skin before using to wash off any residual brine.

Another version of preserving lemons involves adding various spices and herbs such as bay leaves, cinnamon sticks, coriander seeds, cumin, black peppercorns, cloves and red chilis. As before, top up the jar to the brim with fresh lemon juice at the start of the preserving process.

Sweet oranges are also very popular. They only came to Europe after the discovery of the sea passage to India. From Europe, the trees were first exported to North Africa, from where they spread steadily east. They are customarily simply peeled and eaten fresh, and also divided into segments and used in fruit and other salads.

Bananas

Banana cultivation was practised in the early Islamic period in Mesopotamia. In the opinion of some translators, bananas are mentioned among the fruits of Paradise listed in Surah 56, verse 29 of the Qur'an. Islamic conquests in India led to a further expansion in the cultivation of bananas. By the 8th century they were widespread throughout the eastern part of the Islamic world. In the following century, their cultivation in Egypt is documented. By the 19th century, they were also familiar trees in the environs of Jerusalem. It was almost certainly from Egypt that banana cultivation spread to North Africa, where they are mentioned in historical sources from the 11th century. However, because they were also present in Spain a century before, it is fair to assume that they existed in North Africa well before this date. The fruit from the southeast coast of Spain was regarded at that time as the best banana crop in the entire Arab world. Banana trees were also planted in Oman as early as the 10th century. From there, they spread to East Africa, especially Zanzibar. The renowned Arab world traveller Ibn Battuta came across them in Mogadishu and Mombasa in the 14th century. He reported that the fruit formed the staple diet of the local populace in those regions; the bananas were cooked while still green and then spiced with ginger and mango. There is no clear evidence to indicate whether bananas reached Sub-Saharan Africa by being transported inland from the East African coast or instead were taken on the trade routes across the Sahara from North Africa. In any event, the Portuguese certainly encountered them during the voyages of exploration in the 15th century. As a rule, bananas were and still are primarily used in the Middle East in fruit desserts, often in conjunction with other raw fruit or as an element in a fruit salad. Yet a few recipes using bananas as their main ingredient can be found in medieval Arabic cookbooks.

Jūdhāba with bananas

This recipe from al-Warraq's cookbook is attributed to the Abbasid ruler Prince Ibn al-Mahdi (d. 839).

Peel bananas and set them aside. Place a *ruqāqa* (a round, thin flatbread) in a shallow ovenproof dish or pan and top it with slices of banana. Sprinkle the banana pieces with pure cane sugar and lay another *ruqāqa* on top. Continue layering flatbreads, bananas and sugar until you have filled the dish. Pour sufficient rosewater over the contents of the pan to soak everything well through. Place the dish in a medium-hot oven *(tannūr)* and bake. Hang a chicken in the hot oven above the banana dish and let it roast till golden-brown, *inshallāh.*

Water melons

The antecedents of the water melons that are now such a well-loved fruit throughout the Middle East came from the veldts and savannas of Africa. The first mention of water melons and wall-painting depictions of them come from Pharaonic Egypt. They are thought to have been taken from Egypt to Palestine and to West Africa. They can still be found in both these locations today, growing in a semi-wild form. The form of water melon that we are familiar with nowadays was almost certainly first native to India. From there it found its way at a relatively late stage – namely in the 8th century – to China. In the literature written by Muslim authors of the Middle Ages, melons are first mentioned in the context of eastern regions such as Mesopotamia. By the 12th and 13th centuries, water melons were widespread in Egypt, where they enjoyed particularly favourable growing conditions. In the 13th century, the geographer al-Qazwini (1203–1283) reported that the melons produced in Upper Egypt were so large that a camel could not carry more than two of them. It is also safe to assume from the fact that the cultivation of water melons is treated in Andalusian farming manuals of the 11th and 12th centuries that the fruit must have been grown in North Africa at the same time or even earlier. Yet the first reports of it from the region only date from the 14th century, and these claim that it was not very commonly found there. There are also accounts of water melons being grown in Yemen and Ethiopia at around the same time. As is the case today, water melons were always eaten fresh, with their high water content providing welcome refreshment especially in the summer months.

Spinach

The 'queen of vegetables', as the Andalusian agricultural teacher Ibn al-'Awwam called spinach, was unknown in Classical Antiquity in Europe. It is first documented in pre-Islamic Iran, from where it was also taken to Nepal. Around 647, first mention is made of it in China, where it was still known as 'Persian greens'. Its spread to Europe occurred along Arab trade routes. The first Arabic texts in which it is identified by name are those of the Persian physician Muhammad ibn Zakariya al-Razi (864–925) and the Iraqi agriculturalist Ibn Wahshiyya.

This vegetable warrants no special mention in the works of later geographers and travellers, no doubt because it was by then so widely distributed. It was a different story in Spain, however, where a series of authors of agricultural textbooks such as Ibn Bassal (c. 1085) describe spinach and its cultivation. Indeed, one book (c. 1074) by the Andalusian author Ibn Hajjaj even deals with nothing but the cultivation of spinach, another indicator of how widespread it must have been by then. As in modern Arabic, Iranian and Turkish cookbooks, medieval collections of recipes offer a whole host of suggestions on how to prepare spinach.

Spinach reached Italy from the Middle East as early as the 11th century. At the famous medical school of Salerno (*Schola Medica Salernitana*), an institution that played a key part in transmitting Arab medicine to the West, it was taught that lentils became more digestible through the addition of spinach. However, spinach only became more widely available and commonplace in the West in the 16th century; at that stage, the route by which it came to Italy was evidently via Spain and France. In German cookbooks of this period, spinach is still being treated as a form of medication, as it had been in Salerno. It was deemed to have health-giving properties especially in cases of stomach or bowel disorders, but also against kidney stones and even to alleviate respiratory problems. Its seed was used to treat jaundice. However, it was not until the beginning of the 20th century that it began to play a more significant role in the kitchen. Once more, it was initially a health aspect that was decisive in this development. Spinach was erroneously assumed to have a greater iron content than other vegetables and hence that it was especially beneficial to children and adolescents. In the meantime, spinach has gained greatly in popularity for its subtle flavour, even though this enthusiastic reception is not shared by many children.

Spinach and lamb stew

This recipe can be found in the medieval cookbook of al-Tujibi.

Take as much meat as you wish from a young, plump wether. Cut it into small pieces and wash carefully before placing it in a new (earthenware) pot. Add salt, olive oil, pepper, ground coriander seed and a small amount of finely chopped onion. Put the pot over a flame and shake it vigorously until the meat has browned all over and the juices have begun to run. Cover the meat with boiling water. Now take a bunch of spinach and select for preference the youngest, tenderest leaves. Put them in a clean, separate pan with a splash of water and put it over a flame. When it starts to boil, take it off the heat, drain and tip the spinach onto a plate. Mash it with the blunt side of a knife until it is finely chopped and has taken on the consistency of dough. When you can see that it is ready, add some herbs of your choice to it. Blend a lump of butter or other fat with chopped coriander leaves and peppermint and add this to the spinach. Now combine the meat and the spinach and let the pot simmer for a while longer over a low heat. To serve, decant the meat and spinach onto a large dish and crumble over some crumbled fresh goat's or sheep's cheese if you like.

As early as the 13th century, spinach had come to Europe via Andalusia and quickly supplanted the then-popular orache (a herb of the goosefoot family). Medieval cookbooks contain almost no recipes for spinach. This may have been because the vegetable was too commonplace to be worthy of inclusion in a cookbook. In his work *De honesta voluptate et valetudine* ('On Honourable Pleasure and Health', c. 1465) the librarian at the Vatican Library Bartolomeo Platina gave the vegetable a very favourable write-up: 'Spinach is the lightest form of garden vegetable that one can find. I believe that it can be divided up into two different varieties – black and white. The black variety grows almost with a head like onions, cabbage and lettuce. There is scarcely a garden vegetable that has a wider distribution. Some people are of the opinion that it is ineffectual and has no strength. However, when consumed it can help ease menstruation pains in women… It is also extremely efficacious for those suffering from diseases of the liver and the spleen… It can alleviate the heat of summer, help revive those whom sickness has robbed of their appetite, and fills breastfeeding women with milk. If you eat it along with its juices it will set your bowels in motion. But if you eat it on its own and discard the juices, its effects will be much reduced.'

In its mention of the use of the vegetable with cinnamon and dates, the English cookbook, *The Good Housewife's Jewel* by Thomas Dawson (1596), hints even more strongly at the Arab origin of spinach:

How to make egg dough with spinach

Take a good amount of spinach (300 grams, say) and wash thoroughly to remove all traces of dirt and grit. Simmer in a splash of clean water. When it has cooked and wilted remove the spinach from the pan and drain it in a colander. When it is cool enough, squeeze the reduced ball of cooked spinach between your hands to squeeze out as much residual moisture as you can. Then chop finely with the blunt side of a knife. Finally add beaten eggs and breadcrumbs. Season the dough with sugar, cinnamon, ground ginger and pepper. To complete the dish, stir in a handful of finely chopped dates and currants.

In modern times, spinach is served as a salad in the Arab world, as well as in combinations with many other ingredients. For instance, rice is mixed with spinach, or it is combined with chicken or fried eggs; it is also used as a filling for filo or puff pastries, made into soups or mixed with yogurt.

Spinach with chickpeas

Slice 1 large onion thinly and fry in olive oil until browned and caramelised. Then sweat 3 coarsely chopped garlic cloves in olive oil and add to it 250 grams spinach. Fresh, thoroughly washed spinach takes just a few minutes to cook; if you are using frozen spinach instead, follow the instructions for cooking on the packet. Season with salt and pepper and the skin of one preserved lemon cut into very small pieces. Drain a 400 millilitres can of chickpeas and add this and the caramelised onions and the spinach mix. Warm through before serving lukewarm or cold.

Aubergines

Scarcely any vegetable enjoys as much popularity in the region between the Indian Subcontinent in the East and the Atlantic coast as the aubergine. It conquered the northern shores of the Mediterranean a long time ago, and has since taken in large swathes of land north of the Alps. The aubergine, more or less in the form in which we know it today, almost certainly originated in India, and arrived in China in around the early 6th century. The Arabs first got to know about it during their campaign of conquest in Iran. Ibn Wahshiyya said of the vegetable: 'It is a plant from Persia that has spread to all parts of the world.' By the 10th century at the latest, the aubergine had established itself as a favourite food throughout the Arab world. It appeared not only in treatises on farming but also in pieces of literature and collections of poetry. From the East, the aubergine then embarked on its triumphal march westward, reaching Spain, where its cultivation is discussed in agricultural texts from the 10th to the 13th century. Historical documents from the 14th century indicate that it was by then present in both Ethiopia and the West African Muslim state of Kanem. In view of the lively interest shown in this exotic vegetable by farming manuals, it comes as little surprise to find that a great deal of information exists from this period on the different varieties of aubergine.

Even Ibn Wahshiyya named six different types varying in both shape and colour, while the Spanish Moorish writer Ibn al-'Awwam mentioned four varieties, including one native to his local region which was known as the Córdoba aubergine. The elongated form of aubergine allegedly baffled a Chinese traveller to Samarkand in 1221, since he was only familiar with the round sort available in his homeland. A report from 14th-century Yemen spoke of a white aubergine that supposedly originated from China. It was evidently something quite special as it was growing in the garden of the Yemeni ruler.

There are now an incalculable number of aubergine recipes; this is down to the aubergine's ability to combine well with the most diverse of flavours. It is cooked as an appetiser, a vegetable side dish and in combination with meat, especially chicken. The only place where it plays no role whatsoever is in dessert recipes.

Aubergine Purée with mint and almonds

Aubergine purées are favourite starters; they can be found in every Arab mezze selection, under the names of *moutabal* or *baba ghanoush*. Here is an original Turkish version.

Roast two large aubergines over a charcoal grill or – as has latterly become the traditional norm – directly over the gas flame of a hob burner until the skin is blackened and the flesh has turned soft. During cooking, the aubergines need to be constantly turned for every side to be cooked. When they have cooled sufficiently, scoop the flesh from the burnt skins (discard the latter) and chop it as finely as you can. Put the chopped flesh into a large bowl and mix with the juice of half a lemon, 3 crushed garlic cloves, 1 tablespoon pomegranate molasses, 3 tablespoons roughly chopped almonds, a handful of chopped fresh mint, salt and freshly ground black pepper, and mix thoroughly. Taste and adjust seasoning to taste. The resulting purée can be garnished with some small mint leaves and a sprinkling of toasted pine kernels for serving.

Another outstanding dish with aubergines as its main constituent is *Ali Nazik Kebab*.

Ali Nazik kebab

Grill 3 aubergines (total weight 750 grams) over an open flame until all sides are evenly done and the vegetables have taken on a smoky flavour. Scrape the flesh from the charred skins, put it in a pan and continue to soften over a low heat. When the aubergine is thoroughly cooked, remove from the pan and place in a fine-meshed sieve for several hours to allow the bitter juices to drip out. Meanwhile in a medium pan heat a little olive oil and when it is hot fry 250 grams of lamb or beef mince until browned. Add to this 1 small tin chopped tomatoes and season generously with salt and pepper. Over medium heat boil off all the excess moisture, then take off the heat and allow to rest. In a large bowl, mix around 200 grams plain yoghurt with 4 cloves of pressed garlic with a pinch of salt. Return the aubergine purée to a clean pan and reheat with butter before stirring in the yoghurt and garlic mix. Turn this out onto a dish, top with the fried minced meat and serve immediately.

This recipe is now to be found throughout Turkey, though it is said to have originally come from Gaziantep. A similar dish exists in Iran. As to who Ali Nazik was, Turkish families have been arguing over this for generations without ever coming to a conclusive answer.

At first, aubergines were not very highly regarded in the West. Though they were used frequently in the cookery of Moorish Spain (al-Andalus), after the Reconquista only a very few dishes involving aubergines appear in the cuisine of Catalonia. Likewise, in Sicily under Muslim rule the vegetable was not so popular among Christians on the island.

There was a general assumption that these strange, in some cases egg-shaped, plants were poisonous. Sometimes they were confused with tomatoes; certainly, both were referred to as *pomodori* in Italy. In the second half of the 15th century, the Italian culinary expert Martino da Como still felt it necessary to explain how to deal with aubergines:

How to prepare aubergines so that they are neither too strong nor unpalatable

Cut them into quarters and carefully peel them. Then bring a little salted water to the boil. When the water begins to boil, put in the aubergine pieces and let them cook for the duration of two 'Our Fathers'. Remove from the water and let them dry. Coat them with flour and fry them like fish. When they are cooked through, pour off most of the excess oil while still leaving a little in the pan with the aubergines. Then mash up a clove of garlic with one-quarter of the aubergines. Take a pinch of oregano of the kind you normally sprinkle on anchovies and crush this with a little more garlic and some breadcrumbs, saffron, pepper and salt. Moisten this mixture with a splash of verjuice, or if you find verjuice too strong, use water instead. Tip this all into the pan with the fried aubergines and cook for a short while. Turn out onto a flat plate and serve hot.

From the Middle East to Europe

Many ingredients for Middle Eastern cookery have also spread into the Christian West by a variety of routes. Over time, merchants and crusaders brought this or that culinary idea or practice back with them to Northern Europe.

The Iberian Peninsula and the Balkans, for example, witnessed a lively exchange of plants, fruit and knowledge about how to cultivate and prepare them. The dietary textbooks by authors writing in Arabic, which were translated into Latin principally in Italy, played a key role. They helped acquaint people with various spices, fruits and types of vegetable that were unknown in Europe hitherto. The names of a whole range of foodstuffs and beverages betray their Middle Eastern origins. A few of these are discussed below:

Alcohol

It is one of the crowning ironies of the history of culinary transfer from the East to the West that any alphabetically organised list of ingredients would begin with the word 'alcohol', in other words with one of the very things that Islamic law has decreed taboo. In Arabic the word *al-kuhl* means 'antimony powder', used for darkening eyelids, a purpose which it still serves today. Variants of the word point to the fact that this make-up technique was already being practised in India, in the civilisations of the ancient Far East, and in pre-Islamic times on the Arabian peninsula. In addition to its cosmetic purpose, *al-kuhl*, also known as *kohel* (kohl) was a remedy against eye infections. Even nowadays the (mistaken) conviction is widespread across large sectors of Arab society that kohl protects against ocular diseases. Accordingly, antimony powder is put into the eyes of small children. By contrast, the practice of making up the eyes with kohl only became established in the West in the 20th century. Yet it had first been recognised as an active therapeutic substance as early as the 12th century. The extraordinary fineness of antimony powder was often compared to solar dust. Thus it was that the Swiss physician and mystic Paracelsus (1493–1541) applied the term to the finest of wines (*alcohol vini*) for the first time in 1527. The technique of distillation – which was already known about in the Ancient East and in Classical Antiquity – was improved by Arab alchemists and physicians, for instance as a method of producing rosewater.

Rose petals were heated up in an alembic with a little water, and the cooled steam that resulted was condensed and transformed into rosewater. However, the Arabs never attempted to distil wine. It was the Strasbourg alchemist and doctor Hieronymus Brunschwig (1450–1512) who first successfully applied the techniques of distillation to wine. Alcohol became a therapeutic elixir, manufactured primarily by apothecaries. Yet even as late as the 18th century, the term 'alcohol' was still being used to denote a very fine powder.

Apricots

The apricot has come down to us via a very particular culinary route. It was domesticated as early as the 1st century AD in Italy, where it was referred to as the 'Armenian apple' (*malum Armeniacum*). Following the collapse of the Western Roman Empire in the 5th century, widespread cultivation of the apple largely fell into oblivion. However, Arab farmers continued to grow apricots. At the beginning of the 16th century no fewer than sixteen different varieties of the fruit are said to have existed in Northern Morocco alone. The Classical Arabic name for the apricot is *al-barqūq*, although the word *mish-mish* is in far more common usage – however, the same word is also used for peaches. The original High Arabic word *al-barqūq* gave rise to the range of words used in various Romance languages, such as *albaricoque* (Spanish), *abricot* (French) and so on. Apricots can be found in numerous Arab and Persian cookbooks, where they are used not just in desserts but also in meat and even fish dishes. Such savoury combinations are especially popular in Persian and Moroccan cookery. Many recipes use dried apricots. In Iran and Turkey, after harvesting, the ripe, stoned fruit are laid out on the flat roofs of houses in the sun and carefully monitored. When they have reached a certain stage of desiccation, they are packed in sacks and stored.

Lamb with apricots

As so often is the case, there are many different versions of this stew, or *khoresh* in Farsi. This version comes from the city of Kashan in central Iran.

Chop 2 large onions finely and sweat them in a large pan until they are translucent. Add 1 teaspoon ground turmeric and 500 grams lamb shoulder cut into 2-centimetre cubes and brown in the oil. Now put in 100 grams of washed red lentils and fry with the meat and onions for another 5 minutes. At the end of this cooking time, add 200 grams stoned and dried apricots cut into quarters, 5 crushed saffron threads soaked in a little warm water, a pinch of grated nutmeg, salt and pepper. Pour 125 millilitres boiling water into the pot and quickly bring back to the boil. Then reduce the heat, cover and simmer gently for 2 hours. At the end of cooking add a little hot water if the mixture seems too dry, though remember that *khoresh* is meant to be a thick stew. Serve with plain yoghurt.

❧ ❧ ❧ ❧ ❧ ❧ ❧ ❧ ❧ ❧ ❧ ❧ ❧ ❧ ❧ ❧ ❧ ❧

North African cuisine is also fond of combining apricots with lamb:

Tagine with apricots

In a tagine or flameproof casserole, mix together 1 kilogram lamb shoulder cut into largish chunks, 4 chopped onions, 4 crushed garlic cloves, 1 level teaspoon ground cinnamon, a small piece of peeled and finely grated root ginger, 1 level teaspoon ground turmeric, chopped flat-leaf parsley, 1 teaspoon ground coriander seeds, salt and pepper and fry in a mixture of butter and oil for 5 minutes. Once the pieces of meat have browned, cover the contents of the tagine with hot water and leave to simmer for 45 minutes over a moderate heat.

Top up regularly with hot water to prevent the mixture from becoming too dry. After 30 minutes' cooking time, ladle out some of the liquid in the tagine and combine this in a separate small pan with 200 grams quartered dried apricots and cinnamon plus a little sugar and a pinch of salt. Cover this pan and simmer over a moderate heat for 15 minutes. Again add water while cooking if necessary. Remove the apricot pieces from the pan and allow to drain. As soon as the lamb in the tagine is tender, lift out the pieces of meat and keep them warm; boil the remaining liquid to reduce it to a thick consistency and pour over the warmed lamb, then finish by sprinkling with the stewed apricots. The ideal accompaniment for this dish is plain couscous.

✳ ✳ ✳ ✳ ✳ ✳ ✳ ✳ ✳ ✳ ✳ ✳ ✳ ✳ ✳ ✳ ✳ ✳

Coffee

Any coffee aficionado who has ever ordered a bag of Arabica beans or a cup of mocha and paused to think about the derivation of these terms will soon have hit upon the fact that coffee – the world's most popular and widespread hot beverage – has its roots in Arabia and East Africa. *Coffea arabica* ('coffee shrub of Arabia') was a plant endemic to the mountainous regions of Yemen on the Arabian Peninsula and highlands of Ethiopia and is believed to have been the first species of coffee to be cultivated. The term 'mocha', meanwhile, comes from the name of a port in southwestern Yemen, al-Mukha in Arabic, which in the 17th century became the sole point of export for this increasingly sought-after commodity. A host of theories have been put forward, many of which do not stand up to historical scrutiny, concerning the route by which this stimulating drink came to enter the European consumer culture. The Arabic word for coffee is *qahwah*. Yet at the same time this was one of the 150 different Arabic terms for 'wine'. Only in the 16th century was the term used for the new drink that had begun to arrive in the Near and Middle East from Yemen or Ethiopia. Shepherds are reputed to have noticed that their sheep and goats became particularly agitated after browsing on the leaves of a particular species of bush. Then it is said that Islamic Sufi mystics prepared a brew from the beans (a word that itself derives from Arabic, *bunn*) of the bush, which allegedly made it easier for them to conduct and endure their long nocturnal observances. From Yemen, coffee beans were transported to Cairo via Mecca and by the 16th century had even reached Istanbul. There, scholars of Sharia law discussed whether this new drink was an 'inadmissible innovation' or not.

In the course of these legalistic wranglings, it is quite likely that the fact that its name had once been a poetic designation for wine played a role. In any event, the critical attitude of the official institutions of the Ottoman state stemmed from the worry that opposition forces might meet and conspire in the newly emerging coffee houses and, under the guise of drinking coffee, hatch plans against the prevailing order. As a result, public coffee drinking was subject to repeated bans.

It was only in the 18th century, with the introduction and spread of coffee as a permitted stimulant, that premises developed that could be visited by Muslims without any moral misgivings. According to accounts given by European travellers, the atmosphere in these establishments was calm and almost contemplative. Apart from the necessary orders to the serving staff, the main sound to be heard in these places was that of storytellers reading fairy tales or popular novels aloud. In doing so they would sit on a raised dais and accentuate their performances with animated gestures. Evidently, another well-established form of entertainment was for travellers to recount their experiences in foreign lands. Above all, from the 18th century onwards, in many regions of the Middle East coffee houses became meeting points for the upper echelons of society, and in the 19th and 20th centuries principally for the literati in the major cities of the Near and Middle East. In consequence, a kind of coffee-house culture arose. Groups of literary figures, journalists and other freelance professionals would meet daily at a particular time in a particular coffee house in order to discuss burning issues of the moment, to listen to the recordings of famous musicians and singers (especially divas) on the newly developed phonographs, and to compose their own works, like the Egyptian Nobel Prize winner Naguib Mahfouz (1911–2006), who wrote some of his most important works in coffee houses.

Coffee in the Turkish manner

The brewing of Turkish coffee is widespread throughout the Middle East. To make it requires a long-handled pot known as an *ibriq* or a *cezve*. Into this put enough water to make two small cups (demitasses) of coffee. On the hob, bring the pot slowly to the boil and when it starts to simmer, add sugar to taste. There are three degrees of sweetening: heavy, medium and light. Most people nowadays prefer medium-sweet. When the water has returned to a rolling boil, take the pot off the stove and add 4 heaped teaspoons of (2 per person) of very finely ground coffee. A teaspoon or so of ground cardamom may also be added to give the authentic taste of Turkish coffee, or cinnamon if you prefer. Bring back to just below boiling point. Once the coffee begins to foam, remove the pot from the heat and rap it down gently but firmly on a pad or wooden board, taking care not to spill the contents, in order to make most of the ground coffee 'sludge' sink to the bottom. Repeat this twice more. Foam will have formed on the surface. Carefully pour the coffee into demitasses with flat bases and serve with glasses of fresh water to cleanse the palate.

Dates or sweets such as Turkish Delight may be served with coffee. Even nowadays, certain magical practices are associated with the Turkish method of preparing coffee. Like the reading of tealeaves, when the coffee has been drunk, the cups are inverted on the saucers and people's fortunes can supposedly be told from the resulting patterns left by the residue.

A long-handled pot is also needed for brewing Arabian coffee. However, the little cups it is served in do not have a flat base, but come to a point, meaning that they cannot be set down. A servant pours coffee in tiny quantities into these cups for immediate drinking. Guests waggle the hand holding the coffee cup to and fro when they do not want it to be refilled. Because of the way it is prepared, Arabian coffee is very bitter, and one seldom drinks more than a couple of sips.

Arabian coffee

To begin with, roast green coffee beans for 20 minutes, ideally over an open fire and turning them constantly during the roasting with a special flat spoon. Grind the roasted beans using a pestle and mortar. The finer the beans are ground, the better the resulting coffee will be. Then, using the same implement, finely grind the black seeds from at least 20 green cardamom pods (discard the husks). Put the coffee, and cardamom to taste, in a pot filled with cold water and slowly bring the mixture to the boil. As soon as it begins to froth, decant it into a pot with a spout and serve it to your guests.

The earliest coffee houses in Europe were established from the mid-17th century on, notably in Venice, Marseilles and Oxford. The first coffee house in London was opened in 1652 by a Sicilian Greek called Pasqua Rosée. Keen to promote his new product, that same year Rosée published a pamphlet entitled 'The Vertue of the Coffee Drink' in which he claimed that coffee is 'good against sore eyes... & will very much stop any defluxion of rheums... & so prevent the cough of the lungs.' Far-fetched though these assertions may be, his claim that it 'will prevent drowsiness & make one fit for business' proved demonstrably true. In the 18th century in particular, coffee houses became an established fixture in the social and intellectual fabric of British life. Men from the arts, the law, politics, journalism, the Church, commerce and the arts gathered there to converse, debate, do business and discuss the issues of the day. The standard price of a penny for a cup of coffee and the great diversity of topics talked about in the coffee houses led to them being referred to as 'penny universities'. Lloyd's Coffee House, which was founded in 1686 by Edward Lloyd, became a venue where members of the booming British merchant industry met to discuss matters of insurance, shipbroking and foreign trade, and over time became the major insurer Lloyd's of London. Leading English and Irish literary figures such as Pepys, Dryden, Pope and Swift were all frequenters of coffee houses.

Until it became fully established in the West, however, coffee-drinking continued to be viewed with suspicion and even open hostility as a degenerate habit of the 'exotic' East. In 1599, while on his way to Persia, the English Jacobean adventurer Sir Anthony Sherley gave a highly disparaging sketch of life under Ottoman lands: 'damned infidels and sodomitical Mahomets [Muslims] … sitting cross-legged for the most part, passing the day in banqueting and carousing until they surfeit, drinking a certain liquor which they do call coffee.'

And when the habit of drinking coffee became widespread, the Christian churches reacted in much the same way as the Ottoman rulers once had, construing the gathering of individuals for conviviality and non-religious interaction as a direct threat to their authority. In the late 16th century, the Vatican described the new beverage as 'Satan's latest trap to catch Christian souls', no doubt simply because of its popularity among Muslims. However, Pope Clement VIII (reigned 1592–1605) is said to have declared on tasting coffee: 'This Satan's drink is so delicious that it would be a pity to let the infidels have exclusive use of it.' In Ethiopia, the original home of the coffee bush, the Ethiopian Orthodox Church proscribed coffee drinking from the 12th century onwards as a 'vile' Muslim habit, a heretical act equivalent to smoking tobacco or chewing the narcotic leaf *qat*. This ban lasted until 1889 when Emperor Menelik II, who had developed a personal liking for coffee and besides was keen to boost the export of home-grown beans, overturned it.

Likewise, secular rulers were afraid of the no-holds-barred political debate and lobbying that went on in coffee houses. A proclamation issued by King Charles II in 1675 maintained that these establishments had given rise to 'very evil and dangerous effects … for that in such Houses … divers False, Malitious and Scandalous Reports are devised and spread abroad, to the Defamation of His Majestie's Government, and to the Disturbance of the Peace and Quiet of the Realm.' Yet the ensuing public outcry demonstrated that the monarch was out of step with public opinion, and coffee continued its triumphal progress. An anonymous poem published in London around the same time as the royal proscription reflected the prevailing mood, hailing coffee as:

'…that Grave and Wholesome Liquor,
that heals the Stomach, makes the Genius quicker,
Relieves the Memory, revives the Sad,
and cheers the Spirits, without making Mad.'

Marzipan

The name of this popular confection made from almonds and sugar does not, as one might possibly surmise, derive from the Latin *Marci panis*, meaning 'bread of St. Mark'. Yet the association between marzipan and Venice is nonetheless not entirely spurious. Even in pre-Islamic Iran there was a delicacy which was known in Arabic as *lauzīnaj*; the Arabic word for 'almond' is *lauz*. According to recent studies, the word 'marzipan' is now almost certainly thought to relate to a measure of capacity, known as a *matapan*, which was used on Cyprus in the 14th century. This may well have an etymological connection to an Arab term for cases or vessels made of glass or earthenware jars for preserves, which could also be used for storing precious items such as pearls or expensive spices.

In any event, the name of the container transferred over time to its contents; shifts like this can also be identified in several other Arabic words that became European concepts.

Lauzīnaq (also known as Lauzīnaj)

Several different versions of this medieval recipe can be found in the cookbooks by al-Warraq and al-Tujibi.

Take a quantity of cornstarch, add enough egg white to make a thick paste and strain through a sieve; use 1 egg white for every 30 grams of starch and stir the mixture constantly. Heat a flat skillet and rub it with a wax cloth and some shelled walnuts. Once it is hot, put a little of the mixture into the pan. When the (thinly spread) 'bread' is ready, scrape it off the pan and set aside. Clean the pan as before and make another piece until you have used up all the paste. Now take some shelled almonds and walnuts, plus an equal quantity in weight of sugar. In a pestle and mortar grind the two kinds of nut separately until fine; do the same with the sugar, then combine them and bring the mixture together with a splash of rosewater. Add a touch of musk, amber and gum mastic, all finely ground beforehand. Then crush some more almonds and walnuts to extract their oils. Pour the nut oil into a glass jar and set aside. Now take the pliable sheets of *lauzīnaq* 'bread' and spread each of them generously with the nut mixture, topping with another sheet. Cut these into smaller pieces of a size that suits you best. Carefully place the filled pieces of *lauzīnaq* into a wide-mouthed jar made of green-glazed earthenware or glass until the jar is almost full, then pour over the reserved nut oil to cover. This preserved confection can be eaten on journeys or used in the home.

Saffron

Saffron must surely be the world's most expensive spice. It consists of the stigmas and styles of a particular species of crocus (*Crocus sativus,* commonly called the 'saffron crocus') that only grows in certain parts of the world, such as certain areas of Yemen and Iran, but also in Tuscany. Picking the crop is extremely labour-intensive. In order to obtain 1 kilogram of saffron, the orange-red stigmas and styles of no fewer than 150,000 flowers are required. This spice is highly prized and frequently used in eastern cuisines. It does not merely serve to impart a beautiful yellow colour to dishes. The Arabs of the pre-Islamic period used saffron for cosmetic purposes. Women painted their eyelids with it, while men used it to colour their beards and hair. In Islamic times saffron was occasionally used as an expressly luxury product to dye fabrics. Increasingly, its medicinal significance came to the fore. Saffron was seen by Arab physicians of the Middle Ages as a remedy for heart problems and nervous aliments and to alleviate menstruation pains. It was also supposed to enhance kidney function, was used to treat eye problems and was even reputed to be an aphrodisiac. By contrast, the recipes in medieval culinary literature not only praise saffron for its ability to lend colour to dishes but also particularly for its delicate flavour. It was mixed with vinegar, honey and above all rosewater. In Iran, where saffron is widely used, there is a popular conviction that it makes people smile. The following recipe for chicken is one of countless Iranian dishes that use saffron as a key ingredient:

✳ ✳ ✳ ✳ ✳ ✳ ✳ ✳ ✳ ✳ ✳ ✳ ✳ ✳ ✳ ✳ ✳ ✳

Morgh-e zaferāni

Cut 500 grams fresh chicken, preferably boneless thighs, into largish pieces and put in a casserole. With a hand blender or in a mixer, blend together 50 millilitres of olive oil, a handful of fresh mint leaves, 3 finely chopped cloves of garlic, 2 tablespoons (!) saffron threads, crushed and steeped in warm water, the finely chopped zest and the juice of 2 lemons, ground cardamom, a good pinch of dried mint, salt and pepper and distribute the resulting paste over the chicken. Leave to marinate for at least 1 hour before placing under the oven grill at a high temperature and cooking for two to three minutes each side.

✻ ✻ ✻ ✻ ✻ ✻ ✻ ✻ ✻ ✻ ✻ ✻ ✻ ✻ ✻ ✻ ✻ ✻

Sorbets

A sorbet, the name of which derives from the Arabic word *shariba* in the sense of 'to drink', was originally a sugar or fruit drink cooled with snow, which first gained widespread popularity during the period of the Abbasid caliphate. Very often, rosewater was mixed with the cold liquid for a more refined taste. It took a considerable logistical effort, not to mention financial outlay, to obtain the snow or ice that was needed to produce these cold drinks even in the height of summer. As a rule, during the Abbasid period, the snow and ice were transported in winter from the mountainous regions of Iran and stored in well-sealed, deep cellars. As the temperature rose with the changing seasons, the price for these coolants steadily increased. The drink known as *sherbet* was also very popular at the late Ottoman court. From the mid-16th century onwards, European – especially Venetian – diplomats and merchants came into contact with it and popularised it in their homelands. Accordingly, it was from Italy that *sorbetto* reached France, where its first appearance as *sorbet* was attested in Paris in the 17th century. The contemporary and increasing vogue for all things Eastern no doubt played an important role in its spread. Not least thanks to constant improvements in methods of refrigeration, sorbets became enormously popular especially in France, where it evolved into the light, semi-frozen water ice that vies in popularity in modern gastronomy with the heavier, egg-custard based ice-creams associated with Italy.

Tomatoes and Peppers – Western Influences on Middle Eastern Cooking

Shifts in international trade

The growth in the military and political strength of the Christian powers from the mid-15th century onwards had many political, social and economic consequences for the countries that lay between the Atlas Mountains in the West and the River Indus in the East. The Europeans brought with them a multitude of practical items and know-how that changed everyday life fundamentally: these included not only implements and technologies but also foodstuffs and new ways of preparing them. The catalyst for this far-reaching change was the fact that Portuguese seafarers discovered the sea passage to India around the Cape of Good Hope. By this route, precious spices began to arrive in Europe directly. As a result, Eastern merchants were deprived at a stroke of their monopoly in this trade, and the revenues earned by Eastern states, which had for centuries been making huge profits in excise duties on these commodities, now suffered a considerable decline. The costs of procuring spices remained immense, but the profits that could be gained in doing so now devolved to European traders. Spices remained well beyond the financial reach of many Europeans and were often only used as medication. A few incredibly wealthy citizens like the Fugger banking family of Augsburg in southern Germany, though, used them to demonstrate their enormous financial clout. For example, Jakob Fugger (1459–1525) is reputed to have burned the promissory notes written to him by the Holy Roman Emperor Charles V (1500–1558) on a fire made of expensive cinnamon sticks. In any event, the monopoly that the East had once held over the commerce in spices was broken by this expansion of trade routes. Above all, the hitherto politically and economically dominant state of Egypt relinquished its former position when the customs revenues on the spice trade suddenly slumped.

The other, equally significant revolution in global trade was the 'discovery' of the Americas in 1492–1493 by a flotilla of Spanish ships commanded by the adventurer Christopher Columbus.

Alongside huge quantities of precious metals, a wide range of plants were sent from the New World to Europe. Many of these plants from the Americas were initially regarded as nothing more than curiosities and were cultivated in the botanical gardens of the European aristocracy. It took several generations for them to find their way into the kitchens and the cooking pots of the Old World. Whenever such plants from the Americas found their way to the East, they were frequently viewed with even greater reserve than had been the case in the West. However, the reasons for this reluctance were much the same in both the East and the West. Unfortunately, very few cultural historians to date have researched the history of the adoption of American crop plants in the Middle East.

American plants in the cuisines of the East

Plants from America were adopted in different ways by the various cuisines of the Middle East. At first, not a single one of these crops was able to establish itself as a staple food, such as happened with the potato in Ireland and Germany. Apart from tomatoes, many American plants still have a certain exotic quality for Middle Eastern cooks. But unlike in Europe, where the Churches, at least in part, took a critical view of these imports, Muslim scholars made no pronouncements about American agricultural crops, because they operated by the principle that plants which did not induce intoxication were to be regarded in general as *halāl*.

In the various comprehensive works that have been written on the global history of food and drink, there is a more or less tacit consensus that economically useful plants from America came to the different regions of the Middle East via Europe and above all in conjunction with modern colonisation movements. When a plant or its fruit was given a name like 'Turkie wheat' (or its Italian equivalent *grano Turco*) for maize, this labelling was simply meant to signify that the plant in question was of foreign origin, not to denote that it actually came from Turkey. It is hard to refute blanket assertions about the routes by which plants were introduced because the sources that might point to a more nuanced state of affairs have thus far barely been explored. Nevertheless, in his outstanding 1994 essay, 'From the Caucasus to the Roof of the World: A Culinary Adventure', the eminent Iran scholar and expert on the history of Middle Eastern food and drink, Bert G. Fragner, has ascertained that, at least in the Ottoman Empire, American plants became known almost simultaneously with their distribution in Europe. According to Fragner's researches, the plants were first brought to Spain and then spread farther to the East via North Africa. Another direct route was fostered by the good relations that existed at the time between Madrid and Istanbul. Certainly, there appears to have been hardly any delay in the spread of these plants.

Potatoes

Despite the fact that the principal area of cultivation of the potato in South America, the High Andes, was reached by the Spanish conquistador Francisco Pizarro as early as 1532, it took another 40 years for potatoes to arrive in Europe. The story of how the plant was first regarded as a curiosity is well known. In the 17th century, potatoes began to be cultivated as a food crop in Ireland and Lower Austria. They gradually spread to other parts of Europe over the course of the 18th and early 19th centuries. Royal or state edicts helped promote the cultivation of the potato as a cheap form of sustenance. Potatoes were very versatile. They could also be used as cattle fodder or distilled into a high-proof alcohol. In southern Europe, however, the potato continued to be held in low esteem and was only used in the kitchen as a form of vegetable. The potato only really became widely known in Italy with the publication in 1891 of a cookbook by Pellegrino Artusi (1822–1911), though it never attained great popularity there.

The potato was somewhat delayed in reaching the Middle East. A report from Istanbul by the Prussian military instructor and later field marshal Helmuth von Moltke in 1835 mentions potatoes. The earliest printed Ottoman cookbook, entitled *Melce üt-tabbahīn*, likens potatoes to Jerusalem artichokes. Meanwhile, the first specific information concerning the spread of the potato in Mesopotamia comes from 1886. The Ottoman authorities governing the province of Mosul promoted the growing of potatoes and offered special bonuses as a reward to farmers who sowed this crop. However, it is fair to assume that similar initiatives were also undertaken in other regions of the Ottoman Empire. The expansion of the Anatolian Railway witnessed an influx of German engineers and advisors to Turkey, who founded the country's first experimental field station for potato cultivation at Adapazari, subsequently replicated at other sites further along the line. As a result of a succession of poor wheat harvests in the 1880s and above all in the wake of the great famine of 1887, potato growing was further intensified in the Ottoman Empire. Cookbooks which date from the 1950s and come from former Ottoman provinces thus contain a number of potato recipes, some of them extremely sophisticated. A very popular method of preparing vegetables in the Middle East is to stuff them; potatoes are also frequently served in this way.

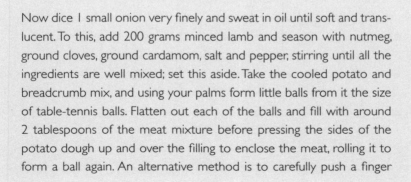

Potato chap

Boil 1.5 kilograms of potatoes in their jackets until tender, then drain off the water and once they are cool enough to handle, peel off the skins. Press the peeled potatoes through a potato ricer, add 3 tablespoons white breadcrumbs and a twist of salt and pepper. Mix thoroughly. If the dough turns out to be too dry, add 1 beaten egg and beat it firmly into the mix. Put the potato dough aside when ready.

Now dice 1 small onion very finely and sweat in oil until soft and translucent. To this, add 200 grams minced lamb and season with nutmeg, ground cloves, ground cardamom, salt and pepper, stirring until all the ingredients are well mixed; set this aside. Take the cooled potato and breadcrumb mix, and using your palms form little balls from it the size of table-tennis balls. Flatten out each of the balls and fill with around 2 tablespoons of the meat mixture before pressing the sides of the potato dough up and over the filling to enclose the meat, rolling it to form a ball again. An alternative method is to carefully push a finger or thumb into each potato ball to make a hollow that you then fill with meat before closing up the hole once more. Press down gently on the filled potato balls to form slightly flattened cakes. Put each finished potato cake carefully to one side and cover with a clean tea towel. In a heavy-based frying pan, heat 4–5 tablespoons sunflower or groundnut oil. When the oil is very hot, put three or four of the cakes into the frying pan (leaving plenty of room to turn them) and brown them lightly on both sides, long enough to ensure that the meat filling is cooked through. Immediately pat the finished cakes dry on some pieces of absorbent kitchen paper. Serve hot. If you do not want to fry all the potato cakes at once, they can be kept for up to 2 days, covered, in the fridge before cooking.

The term 'chap' in this Iraqi-Arab recipe is a loan-word from English; it is thought to be a corruption of the word 'shape'. This recipe is a prime example of how a typically Iraqi dish was adapted to incorporate an ingredient new to the region.

Looking through all the many Arab, Persian, Kurdish and Indian Muslim cookbooks that have been produced, it becomes clear that the potato has still not managed to establish itself as a staple food. Precedence is still given to grain products such as bread, couscous or rice. Potatoes often appear in combination with other types of vegetables. Of course, processed potato products such as crisps and French fries have inevitably made their way into many Middle Eastern households in recent decades.

The familiar Iranian combination of meat and fruits has also been supplemented by potatoes. The following recipe shows that the relatively taste-neutral potato can be used effectively to bulk out many casserole dishes.

Tāskabāb-e ālūkhoshk

Cut 500 grams lamb in 2-centimetre cubes. Cut 5 peeled potatoes into thin slices, likewise 2 large onions and coarsely chop 1 large quince (peeled and cored). Spread the onion rings evenly over the bottom of a heavy-based casserole and add 1 cup of cold water and 4 tablespoons sunflower or groundnut oil. Now create successive layers using half of all the ingredients: the sliced potatoes, the lamb, the quince pieces and 100 grams dried and stoned prunes. Season with cardamom, cinnamon, salt and pepper and pour over the juice of half a lemon. Cover all this with a layer of yoghurt that you have rid of its excess moisture by leaving it to dry out overnight in a lined coffee filter cone. Then repeat the layers with the other half of the ingredients, as before. Finish with a seasoning of pepper, ground turmeric and salt, and once more top with a layer of dried yoghurt. Finally dot the top with small pieces of butter and bake in the oven at a low heat (150°C/ gas mark 2) for one and a half to two hours.

Potatoes are used more frequently in Indian Muslim cookery than in Persian or Arab food. This may be a result of British influence. In any event, a number of potato recipes can be found among the reconstructions of Mughal cuisine. Equally, in view of the intensive contacts that existed between the Mughal rulers and both Italy and Portugal, it is not beyond the realms of possibility that potatoes and other American crops became known in India very shortly after their first appearance in Europe. However, the potato dishes in Mughal cookery do have a distinctively Indian character. Small deep-fried potato patties, containing Indian spices and gram (chickpea) flour, are sold widely as street-food snacks in the large cities of Northern India and Pakistan. One particularly original potato dish comes from the hugely popular TV programme hosted by the chef Zubeida Tariq:

Baby potatoes in caramelised sauce

Wash 1 kilogram very small new potatoes and parboil them lightly with their skins on. They should still be quite firm when you take them out of the water. When they are dry, fry them in a *karahi* in very hot oil until they take on a golden-brown colour. Lift the potatoes from the oil with a slotted spoon and put them in a bowl. Decant the hot oil into another pan. Wipe round the *karahi* with a piece of kitchen paper and set it over a fierce flame once more, and tip in the fried potatoes, 2 tablespoons runny honey (or 1 tablespoon sugar), 1 teaspoon finely ground black pepper, 1 tablespoon hot red chili flakes, 2 tablespoons dark soy sauce, 2 tablespoons white wine vinegar, and salt. Keep turning this mixture over a high heat until the honey and soy begin to caramelise. Immediately remove from the hob and pour over the juice of 2 fresh lemons. This dish makes a fine accompaniment to grilled lamb, beef or chicken.

The cooking vessel called *karahi* that is mentioned in the recipe above is a wok-like pan with two looped handles, traditionally made of cast iron (but also now of stainless steel and copper) and used extensively for frying in Indo-Muslim cookery. Any steep-sided pan can be used as an alternative.

Tomatoes

Whereas Middle Eastern cooks are still conscious of the foreign character of green beans and potatoes, tomatoes have been fully assimilated into the kitchens of the East. Cooks along the southern and eastern shores of the Mediterranean have much the same attitude as their Italian counterparts, many of whom are firmly convinced that tomatoes are an ancient Italian crop. In fact, Christopher Columbus himself is said to have personally brought the first example of a tomato plant from the Americas to Spain.

The first successful cultivation of tomatoes is reputed to have been in Spanish-ruled southern Italy, in other words, sometime before 1700, where they were grown as a fruit. Some of the most important tomato varieties available today (notably the San Marzano plum tomato) were cultivated in this same region from the early 20th century onwards. But even prior to this, several different varieties were grown. From Italy, tomatoes were taken to the south of France, where they were given the name *pommes d'or*, from the Italian *pomodori* (literally 'golden apples'). Yet they remained unknown in Paris until 1790. Just a few years thereafter, tomatoes also reached the Middle East. They are mentioned as ingredients in the first Ottoman cookbook, from the year 1844. In 1872, travel guides claimed that tomatoes were being cultivated along the entire length of the Nile Valley. The Arab designation *banadūra* for tomato is likewise cognate with the Italian word *pomodoro*. This hints at one of the routes by which tomatoes came to the Middle East, namely from Italy to Egypt. As early as 1843, green and red tomatoes were being purchased in large quantities as summer vegetables for the Sultan's court. According to the travel journal of an Italian author they were even being cultivated in the Sultan's gardens before 1786. By contrast, tomatoes were still virtually unknown on the Arabian Peninsula throughout the first half of the 20th century, and hence played no significant role in the traditional cuisine of this region. The thesis advanced by the author of a contemporary Arab cookbook that tomatoes were known about in the Middle East from as early as the 16th century cannot be corroborated. It is, however, correct that the use of tomatoes brought about a fundamental change in Middle Eastern cuisines. They became a key means of thickening and adding colour to meat stews, meaning that chefs could now forego the use of nuts or expensive saffron. Tomatoes were also used to lend a touch of tartness to tagines and other dishes in place of fruit juices or syrups. Only in rare instances were tomatoes served as raw salad vegetables. Instead, they tended to have a decorative function. But in most cases they became a constituent ingredient of meat or vegetable dishes. Nowadays, products such as tomato purée and tomato ketchup are extremely popular. The sweetness of these processed foods also plays an important role in the contemporary cuisine of the Middle East.

There are no precise details indicating when the first attempts were made to grow tomatoes in Iran. Having said that, nowadays their main use in Iranian cuisine is in salads, notably the famous 'Shirazi Salad' comprising tomato and cucumber. However, various uses that the new ingredient was put to when it was adopted into Arab cuisine continue to be performed in Iranian cooking by more traditional methods, such as using pomegranate juice. In Turkey, too, fresh tomatoes are used predominantly in salads. They also occasionally play a role as sauces in many meat and vegetable dishes; more often, though, this function is served by tomato purée.

Çoban salatası (Turkish shepherd's salad)

Slice 100 grams mild onions into thin rounds, sprinkle with salt and leave for 5 minutes before rinsing and patting dry with kitchen paper. Spread the onion rings out on a flat plate and then pile on top the following: 500 grams skinned and deseeded tomatoes diced into cubes, 100 grams skinned and diced cucumber, 1 deseeded and finely chopped red chilli, and a handful of flat-leaf parsley, finely chopped. Make a dressing of lemon juice, olive oil and salt and pour it over the salad immediately before serving. You can also add a few large, de-stoned green olives, cut into pieces, and some crumbled or diced sheep's cheese (feta) if you wish.

Basically, in the whole of current Turkish cuisine there is only one recipe in which tomatoes figure in any major way. This is the famous dish known as *imām bayıldı*. This literally translates as 'the imam fainted'. Many Turkish recipe books speculate on the reason as to why the imam of the dish's title – the prayer leader of a mosque congregation – might have fallen into a swoon.

Some commentators take the view that he must have been overwhelmed by the exquisite taste of this dish. Others, however, maintain that the holy man collapsed as a result of overindulgence. Still others attribute it to the rapture he experienced when he smelt the aroma of the dish cooking. The final explanation is that he fainted when he heard how much expensive olive oil was needed to make the recipe. Whatever the case, though, the dish is simple to prepare and provides a quintessential taste of the Middle East.

İmām bayıldı ('The imam fainted')

Blanch 4 medium-sized aubergines in boiling salted water for about 4 minutes. Remove from the water and, when cool enough to handle, halve each aubergine lengthwise and using a sharp-pointed spoon, carefully scrape out most of the flesh from each half, roughly dice it and set it aside. Take 1 large peeled onion and 4 peeled cloves of garlic, chop them finely and sweat them in olive oil until soft. Then add a can of chopped plum tomatoes and the reserved aubergine flesh and season with salt, black pepper, nutmeg, ground cinnamon and cloves and a pinch of chili flakes or powder to taste. Allow this mixture to simmer for 15 mins; if it becomes too wet, boil it more vigorously to reduce the liquid. When you are happy with the consistency, fill the aubergine halves with the mixture. Place the filled halves closely together in a greased porcelain or metal oven dish and drizzle them generously with olive oil. Bake for around 30 minutes in an oven preheated to 200°C/ gas mark 6. While the aubergines are cooking, dry-roast 3 tablespoons pine kernels in a skillet over medium heat for a minute until just golden brown. Take care not to let them burn. Remove the aubergines from the oven, sprinkle with the toasted pine nuts and serve immediately.

Peppers/chillies

In contrast to the other crops from the Americas, bell peppers gained a very quick acceptance in Europe, because they were initially thought to be a variety of the precious black pepper plant of the East Indies. Columbus had brought examples of the fruit of the paprika plant (in botanical terms, a berry) back from his second voyage across the Atlantic (1493–1496). At first, people thought of it exclusively as a spice. By the early 16th century, peppers were widely known throughout Europe, although climatic conditions meant that they could not be grown everywhere. They were used successfully as a remedy for the deficiency disease scurvy; the high vitamin-C content that made them so effective in this role was only discovered later. Sailors from the Ottoman naval fleet were familiar with peppers as early as 1513, and helped spread them throughout the Sultan's dominions. They were introduced to both Hungary and the Arab provinces of the Empire in this way. By the 18th century, the vegetables were widely known and regularly used at the Sultan's court.

In North Africa, paprika played a special role as a spice, especially in its hotter varieties. Even today, travellers to this region can see serried ranks of red pods – that form the basis of the spice paste called harissa – laid out to dry in the sun on the flat roofs of houses. These are said to have been brought by Spanish conquistadors to Europe, whence they found their way to the Maghreb. Harissa is served in the region as an accompaniment to almost all dishes – apart from desserts – to enhance their flavour and piquancy, often accompanied by sliced spring onions and chopped parsley and drizzled with olive oil. There are many different varieties of the paste, but they are uniformly very hot. Several commercial versions of harissa are now produced, and are sold in tubes or tins.

Harissa

In a food processor, or using a hand-held blender, whizz together 100 grams dried red chilli pods (with the seeds kept in) and 500 grams deseeded and quartered red peppers that have had their skins removed until you have a smooth paste. In a frying pan, using just a dribble of oil, fry 1 small, finely chopped red onion, 3 crushed garlic cloves, 1 teaspoon each of ground coriander and ground cumin until the mixture turns a deep brown. Now add the red pepper and chilli paste and the juice of half a lemon. Cook for 10 minutes at a moderate heat, stirring all the while to stop it burning. Remove from the heat and allow to cool, then add olive oil and stir until you have a thick paste. Put in a ceramic or glass container and cover with at least 1 centimetre depth of olive oil. When working with hot chillies, take precautions such as wearing disposable gloves, washing your hands thoroughly after handling the pods, and above all taking care not to rub your eyes!

❧ ❧ ❧ ❧ ❧ ❧ ❧ ❧ ❧ ❧ ❧ ❧ ❧ ❧ ❧ ❧ ❧ ❧

❧ ❧ ❧ ❧ ❧ ❧ ❧ ❧ ❧ ❧ ❧ ❧ ❧ ❧ ❧ ❧ ❧ ❧

Shakshūka

De-seed 4 large red peppers, cut them in half and bake in the oven at 220°C/ gas mark 7 until the skins turn black. Let the peppers cool slightly before sealing them in a plastic food bag; after 10 minutes' steaming in the bag, the skins can be peeled off easily. Using a hand blender, mash the peppers, 30 grams ground almonds, 3 crushed garlic cloves and a pinch of salt into a paste. Place in a high-sided pan with hot olive oil and fry on a low heat. The paste should bubble gently during cooking. Continue heating for 10 minutes, stirring constantly. After this time, remove from the heat and allow to cool. Put in the fridge and cool for 1 hour; remove 30 minutes before serving to bring the shakshūka to room temperature.

❧ ❧ ❧ ❧ ❧ ❧ ❧ ❧ ❧ ❧ ❧ ❧ ❧ ❧ ❧ ❧ ❧ ❧

A red pepper paste known as *shakshūka* is extremely popular, especially in Morocco. There are many different recipes for it. In Palestine, fried eggs are cooked on top of the paste and the dish is served hot. International chefs pride themselves on being able to serve *shakshūka* in several different versions.

The bulbous form of the familiar red bell pepper positively invites chefs to serve it stuffed. There are two fundamentally different variations on this dish: the stuffed peppers are either pickled or roasted in the oven.

Filfil mahshī (Stuffed Arab bell peppers)

First prepare the brine by dissolving 100 grams salt in 1 litre of water. With a pair of kitchen scissors, snip off the stems of the red peppers and then carefully hollow them out from above, taking care to remove all the seeds and membranes inside. Place the peppers in the brine and leave for two days. After this time, remove and rinse them. In a pan, bring to a simmer a quantity of cider vinegar, together with pieces of fresh peeled ginger root, ground dried chillies, curry powder, turmeric, a bay leaf, 5 peeled garlic cloves, and inches of either dried or fresh herbs such as parsley, mint or dill. Let the vinegar mixture cool.

To make the filling for the peppers, mix together 250 grams fresh flat-leaf parsley, finely chopped, plus the same quantity of finely chopped coriander leaf, finely chopped white cabbage and finely diced carrots, along with 125 grams finely chopped onion, 125 grams finely chopped sundried tomatoes, 125 grams finely chopped chives, 1 tablespoon curry powder, 1 teaspoon ground turmeric, 1 tablespoon each of ground cardamom, ground cinnamon and finely ground dried chilli, 2 tablespoons finely chopped root ginger, and half a teaspoon of salt. Stir all the ingredients together until well mixed and fill the peppers with this mixture. Put them into a large preserving jar with a clip-top lid and rubber seal, cover with the vinegar and seal firmly. Leave for at least a week before using.

Pickling vegetables is an old culinary technique that was practised in the Ancient East. Pickled vegetables of all kinds are frequently sold by itinerant street vendors in all the major cities of the Middle East. In Baghdad, all vegetables pickle in vinegar are known as *torshī*, and are a common accompaniment to many dishes served in Iraq.

In Turkey, peppers are customarily prepared with a filling of meat or rice. Those with a filling of minced meat are regarded as the 'genuine' method of preparation, while those stuffed with rice are referred to as *yalanci biber dolması* ('fake stuffed peppers').

Biber dolması

There are, inevitably, numerous different versions of this dish. The following recipe for the filling comes from Istanbul.

Put 400 grams of lamb mince, 1 medium onion cut into thin slices, salt, 1 tablespoon freshly chopped mint, 100 grams washed rice, 100 grams butter, ground black pepper, ground paprika and 100 millilitres meat stock (preferably lamb) in a bowl and mix well. Heat a knob of butter in a pan and gently fry this filling, stirring in frequently. Do not cook the mixture completely but take off the heat when half-done. Take 4 large red bell peppers and slice off the tops at the stalk end to form a 'lid', then using a spoon scoop out the seeds and membranes from inside the peppers. Blanch the peppers in boiling water for a minute or two. Fill the pepper shells with the meat mixture and replace the lids. Stand the peppers upright into a high-sided flameproof pan in which they will fit tightly and pour over 200 millilitres meat stock. Bring slowly to the boil, then reduce the temperature and simmer at a medium heat for 30 minutes until the peppers are tender and cooked through. Serve hot.

Muhamarra

Clean 1 kilogram red bell peppers and cut in half lengthways. Put them on an oiled baking tray and leave them in an oven that has been preheated to 200°C/ gas mark 6 until the skins turn black and begin to blister. When they have cooled just enough to handle, place the pepper pieces in a plastic bag, seal it and then peel the skins off the peppers after about 10 minutes. In a food processor or using a hand blender, whizz together the pepper pieces, 100 grams stale Arab flatbread *(khobez)* torn into small pieces, 1 chopped garlic clove, 125 grams coarsely chopped walnuts, a whole dried chilli crumbled into flakes, the juice of half a lemon, 5 tablespoons pomegranate molasses, 2 teaspoons sugar, 1 tablespoon each of ground cumin, ground cardamom and ground cinnamon, salt and pepper and 4 tablespoons olive oil and blend to a coarse paste. The *muhammara* should be stored in the fridge in a dish covered with clingfilm for at least 8 hours before eating. The paste can be kept in an airtight plastic container in the fridge for up to 5 days.

Muhammara comes from Turkey and is generally served with flatbreads.

In Iran stuffed peppers are filled with a mixture of cooked lentils, rice and minced meat and are cooked not in stock but instead in a tomato sauce consisting of 1 kilogram tomatoes, 50 grams parsley, garlic, a little sugar, vinegar, salt and pepper. It is uncommon to find other methods of preparing peppers.

Maize (Sweetcorn)

There is a particular story behind the introduction of maize to the Middle East. The crop was brought back to Spain by Christopher Columbus in 1493 and shortly afterwards successfully cultivated there. By 1520, maize had reached the South of France, and some ten years later it was being grown in the northern Italian region of Veneto. Soon after it was also to be found in Hungary and the Balkans. Despite this clear provenance in its spread, the crop became known not only as *kukuruz/кукỳруз* in Serbo-Croatian (which scholars have speculated may be a loan word from Ottoman Turkish), but also as *grano Turco* ('Turkish Corn') in Italian and *Türkischer Weizen* ('Turkish Wheat') in German. In any event, by 1574, it was being grown at various locations in the Ottoman Empire, such as the upper reaches of the River Euphrates. Thanks to its high starch content, maize first gained a firm foothold by becoming a cheap substitute for wheat among poorer people. By the mid-19th century, this cereal had also found favour with the middle classes. Nowadays, maize is used throughout the Middle East primarily as a form of starch. However, cornbread is also baked and there are a number of dishes in which white or yellow maize flour forms one of the key ingredients. Repeated mention is made in modern cookbooks of corn-on-the-cob, which is roasted over hot charcoal in a barbecue. The corn cobs can be spread with various different butter mixtures before or after being griddled in this way.

Jerusalem artichokes

Jerusalem artichokes have latterly been making something of a comeback in European and British cuisine, after having been neglected for quite some time. They were known in France from as early as the 17th century. On the one hand, because of a perceived similarity in flavour they were used instead of globe artichokes when these were unavailable. On the other hand, they were also seen as a foodstuff for the common people, who dubbed them '*pommes de terre*'. They made their first appearance in an Ottoman context in a handwritten cookbook of 1565–1566, where they were likewise referred to as 'earth apples' (*tüffāhül-arz*). They were considered a winter vegetable. In the Ottoman cookbook, *Melce üt-tabbahīn*, the recipes involving it are characterised as being typically French. Currently, the vegetable is scarcely known in people's kitchens in the Middle East, though it does appear on the menus of restaurants in international hotels located in the region.

Cacao

Spanish conquistadors first presented Charles V with cacao beans in 1527 in Madrid. However, the courtiers who were offered a drink made from the beans were far from enthralled by it. It was only by the end of the 16th century that the drink managed to gain a large following of ardent devotees. When, in 1569, Pope Pius V pronounced *ex cathedra* that drinking chocolate did not constitute breaking one's fast, people began to enjoy the American import even during Lent without suffering pangs of conscience. In the 18th century, chocolate as a beverage reached the Ottoman Empire. Yet the taste remained a rather exotic pleasure that was indulged primarily in diplomatic circles. The Chaldean monk Ilyas ibn Hanna al-Mausuli, who travelled widely in Central and South America between 1675 and 1683, was almost certainly the first Arab to write about the cacao tree and the chocolate that was derived from its pods: 'In Babahoyo (Ecuador) you can find trees that look like the mulberry. These bear fruit called "cacao", which are used to make chocolate. The pods hang from the trees like melons, growing directly on the trunks. They turn yellow when they are ripe. The pods are harvested and split open. The fruit inside consists of seeds that are as hard as nuts, which are left to dry. Then they are roasted until they resemble coffee beans in colour, aroma and taste. But they are oily, almost soft. The people here then add as much sugar as is needed to make the cacao sweet, along with cinnamon and ambergris. From this mix, they form little patties that they leave to dry out in the shade. These patties are used to make the beverage chocolate, which they drink like coffee. All Christian countries are now familiar with this commodity, which they import from here and then sell on.' It is uncertain whether chocolate arrived in the Ottoman Empire from Italy or France. Certainly, no recipes involving chocolate as an ingredient are to be found in Turkish cookbooks of the 19th century and beyond. It was only in the second half of the 20th century that recipes begin to appear in which it plays a role. These are mostly for cakes of the kind that are also found in European cookbooks. Thus, one can find instructions for making chocolate marble cake or a chocolate glaze for eclairs.

Tea

Alongside coffee, black or green tea is one of the most familiar hot beverages drunk in the Middle East. A glass of tea is a customary way of welcoming someone into your home. As a foreign visitor to this region, one might be tempted to imagine that this is an age-old custom. Yet tea is actually a relatively modern drink for the Near and Middle East, only becoming widespread in the 1920s. On the one hand, the habit of tea drinking spread from Turkey, where it had been known about since Ottoman times, as so-called 'caravan tea' from Central Asia. After the formation of the Turkish Republic by Mustafa Kemal Atatürk, powerful voices arose in the country, calling for economic self-reliance. While coffee was an imported commodity, certain varieties of tea could easily be grown along Turkey's Black Sea coast. With state subvention, tea production in Turkey was increased, to the extent that before long Turkey was able to export tea. In other countries that bordered on the Black Sea, too, such as Azerbaijan and Georgia, successful nationally supported tea-growing programmes were soon instituted. The fact that these countries' tea-drinking culture originated more or less directly from Russia is shown by its frequent preparation in a samovar.

Tea was known in Morocco from a somewhat earlier time. From the beginning of the 19th century onwards, particularly good quality tea from India and China was carried overland on caravans through Russia to the Baltic Sea. It was then shipped on from there to England. But when the transport of tea via the Baltic was temporarily disrupted by the Crimean War of 1853–1856, British merchants started to send tea via the sea route round the Cape of Good Hope, unloading it in Morocco at the ports of Essaouira and Tangier. From there it was shipped onwards to Europe. Moroccans acquired a taste for the green tea, and before long they began mixing it with leaves of fresh mint. In this way, they invented their characteristic national drink.

Doner Kebabs and Falafels – Middle Eastern Cuisine in Europe

Doners and falafels

Hitherto, little was known about how Arab cooking practices came to be adopted in the West, a process that has been going on ever since the Middle Ages. Of course, Spanish Christians living under Moorish rule had assimilated many aspects of the cuisines of their Muslim lords. On Sicily, likewise, many Arab culinary traditions were maintained despite the much shorter period of Muslim rule in that region. Above all, though, from ancient times up to the 19th century, notwithstanding occasional military conflicts, the Mediterranean continued to guarantee a lively cultural exchange between the states around its shores. For as long as the Middle East remained the technologically, medically and also philosophically superior culture, a wealth of inventions and discoveries flowed through the Southern European route into France and even to some extent, via Italy, into the territories controlled by the Habsburg Empire. And from there, this knowledge was passed on to Northern Europe.

Among cultural historians specialising in food and drink it is a matter of dispute whether medieval recipes and those dating from the Renaissance were directly influenced by Middle Eastern models. Some scholars take the view that descriptions of recipes as 'Saracen' do not point to a Muslim provenance but rather are based on linguistic misconceptions. And there may indeed have been some false etymologies at play here. Yet when one looks at the cookbooks of these periods, one finds quite a number of recipes that can be traced back to a Middle Eastern origin, both as regards their ingredients and their method of preparation. As an example of this, it is instructive to juxtapose here an Arab recipe and a recipe from medieval Germany and compare them.

First, a recipe from the 10th-century Arab cookbook of the Baghdadi scholar Ibn Sayyar al-Warraq:

Fish cooked three ways

Scrape the scales off a large fish and gut it in preparation for stuffing. Once you have cleaned the fish, fill its mouth, gills and cheeks with a mixture of finely chopped lemon leaves, apple peel, salt, thyme and rue. Now take a wide strip of cloth (muslin) that has been soaked in water and wrap it three times round the middle of the fish. The cloth should be as wide as two fists and start 4 fingers' width down from the head. Make sure that it is tightly wrapped three times round, otherwise the material will burn and the whole fish will be baked, thus missing the main point of the recipe. Now wrap the lower third of the fish in overlapping strips of linen that have been saturated with oil. This wrapping can be held in place by knotting thin strips of cloth around the middle and tail-end of the linen binding. Put the fish in a preheated oven (tannūr). When it is cooked, remove it and unwind the two cloth bindings. In this way, you will have a fish that has been cooked in three different ways: the head will be baked, the middle section steamed, and the tail portion fried. For each part, prepare an appropriate sauce, so that nobody would suspect that the whole fish was actually cooked in a single piece, God willing.

The following late medieval German recipe from the cookbook (c. 1495) of Master Eberhard (the head cook of Duke Henry III of Bavaria-Landshut) is less complicated, but still clearly follows its Arab model:

If you want to make three or four dishes
out of one fish

If you wish to make three or four dishes out of a single fish while still preserving the illusion that the fish has remained whole, first take a pike or any other fish and cut it into three or four pieces. Lay the first part on a griddle and let it roast. Cook the second part in a mixture of wine and herbs, pickle the third in vinegar and bake the fourth part, the tail, in the oven. At the end of the various cooking processes, the fish should be reassembled, one piece after the other, so it looks like it is still whole: first the head, then the middle section(s), and finally the tail. Sprinkle the whole fish with chopped parsley to hide the joins. Serve portions of a good sauce or vinegar in several separate little dishes. In this way, each of your guests will eat something different, a very novel experience.

Eberhard's basic idea of using a single fish to generate different taste experiences displays a number of remarkable similarities that can be traced back to the superior culinary arts of Arab cuisine. One further example of a dish owing more than just its name to a Middle Eastern archetype can be found in another German cookbook, with the Middle High German title of 'The Book of Good Food' (c. 1350). The use of almond milk and sugar in this recipe is typical of Middle Eastern cuisine:

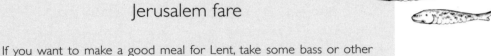

Jerusalem fare

If you want to make a good meal for Lent, take some bass or other suitable fish, immerse them in thick almond milk and cook until tender. Then sprinkle some sugar on top. It is said that this dish is popularly called 'Jerusalem Fare' and can be eaten cold or warm.

In Ibn Sayyar al-Warraq's book there is another recipe that Romance scholars surmise may have been the model for a later Spanish dish, or rather for a method of preparation that derived its name from the original. It is one of the many dishes in medieval Arab cuisine in which vinegar is used.

Sikbāj (al-Warraq's original version)

Cut fat meat [lamb] into middling pieces, place in the pot and cover with water, fresh coriander, cinnamon bark and salt to taste. When boiling, remove the froth and cream with a ladle and discard. Remove the fresh coriander and add dry coriander. Take white onions, Syrian leeks and carrots if in-season, or else aubergine. Skin, splitting the aubergine thoroughly and half-stew in water in a separate pot. Then strain and leave in the pot on top of the meat. Add seasonings and salt to taste. When almost cooked, take wine vinegar and date juice or honey if preferred – date juice is the more suitable – and mix together so that the mixture is mid-way between sharp and sweet, then pour into the pot and boil for an hour. When ready to take off the fire, remove a little of the broth, bray it into the saffron as required and pour it back into the pot. Then

take sweet almonds, peel, split and place on top of the pan, together with a few raisins, currants and dried figs. Cover for an hour to settle over the heat of the fire. Wipe the sides with a clean cloth and sprinkle rosewater on top. When settled, remove from the heat and serve.
[Translation © David Waines, 1989]

The special – and for medieval Middle Eastern cuisine typical – thing about this dish is the mixture of sweetness in the form of date juice or honey and sourness in the form of vinegar. There is a technique in contemporary Spanish cookery in which one steeps meat or fish in a vinegar or citrus juice marinade. This method is known as 'Escabeche'; from Spain it has naturally spread to Mexico, Central and South America.

Escabeche

This recipe naturally has numerous variations.

Slice 2 medium onions into very thin rings and julienne 4 carrots and fry both gently in oil, then add 2 bay leaves, the finely chopped skin of 1 preserved lemon, black pepper, salt, 125 millimetres white wine vinegar and 1 tablespoon sugar. Simmer for 15 minutes over a low heat, then leave to cool. This mixture can be used to marinate chicken but also a range of vegetables like aubergines, red peppers and courgettes.

Poultry

Poultry of all kinds were known about and highly prized in both medieval Europe and the Middle East. There is an unmistakable Middle Eastern flavour about some European recipes involving chicken and other birds. For example, in 1596 in England, Thomas Dawson prepared chicken with grapes, while the French chef Pierre de Lune, whose cookbook was published in 1660, reproduced a recipe that hinted at Arab antecedents, and not just in its name:

Arabian duck soup

Heavily lard a duck and roast it gently. Cut up several turnips into very small pieces and simmer with the duck in hot water until tender. Add salt, pepper, spices and cloves to the broth. Pour some white wine into a small pan and cook two dozen *prunelles* (small, very sharp French plums) in it. After they have softened in the wine and cooled, press them to remove the stones and tip the flesh and juice into a serving dish. Place the cooked duck on top and add some capers and stoned green olives. Press some bread crusts into the plum juice to moisten and soften them, then pour a little lemon juice over the dish. Before serving, garnish with slices of fresh lemon and pomegranate seeds.

Roasting before simmering meat was a cooking technique already well known in Classical Antiquity, which was later practised in Middle Eastern kitchens. On the other hand, one unequivocally Middle Eastern element in the preceding recipe is the combination of duck meat with plums as well as the addition of lemons and pomegranate seeds.

Blancmange

Among the recipes that have been unquestionably identified as originating in Arab cuisine is blancmange. The cultural historian Peter Peter has described this dish as 'omnipresent'. He goes on to explain: 'In present-day France and England, the term is used in a much reduced sense to mean a sweet pudding, whereas in the Middle Ages it was applied indiscriminately to any pale-coloured confection, and in the earliest recipes denoted a very plain dish consisting of chicken meat, sugar, rice and almond milk.' The most famous of these Arab 'blancmange' recipes is *jūdhāba*, a word which according to philologists of medieval Arabic derives from the verb *jadhaba* in its sense of 'to attract' or 'to have an appeal'.

Ibn Razin al-Tujibi, who reconstructed the Muslim cuisine of al-Andalus after the Christian Reconquista, describes the dish as follows:

Jūdhāba

Take one young, plump chicken, pluck and prepare it, cut it open down the breastbone to spatchcock and put it into a pot whole. Add oil, salt, pepper, spikenard, cardamom and water and set it over a fire to cook. Instead of water, you can add a splash of good rosewater if you prefer and cook it without a broth. When the chicken is tender, take two thin flatbreads and lay them in a dish made of stone or earthenware, whose base and sides you have smeared with suet that has been cleaned and manipulated until it has the consistency of marrowbone. Press pieces of flatbread up against the sides of the dish so that they are also completely covered. Sprinkle a spoonful of sugar over each of the flatbreads on the base, together with ground almonds, cloves and spikenard. Drizzle this with a generous amount of olive oil, followed by some more sugar plus rosewater in which a little camphor and musk have been steeped, just sufficient to moisten the sugar. Place one or two more flatbreads on top of this and repeat the procedure of sprinkling them with sugar, almonds and spices and wetting this mixture with rosewater. Carry on with these layers until you have filled half the depth of the dish. Now take the prepared chicken, rub it with saffron that has been soaked in rosewater and place it in the middle of the dish. Cover the spatchcocked bird with more flatbreads and sprinkle these with sugar and almonds as before. Finish the dish by piling up enough flatbreads to fill the dish, with the chicken buried at its centre. On the topmost layer sprinkle a generous amount of sugar and a good helping of oil and rosewater.

Fold down the pieces of bread around the side of the dish to form a tight parcel, then cover the dish securely and seal it with a ring of dough around the rim. Place the *jūdhāba* in a moderately hot oven and leave it there until the chicken is fully cooked through. Remove the dish and break open the flatbread crust to release the full aromas of the meat and spices. If the uppermost breads have been scorched by the heat of the oven, discard them, along with those lining the sides of the dish. Invert the contents of the dish onto a plate and serve immediately.

The 14th-century German *Daz Buoch von guoter Spîse* ('The Book of Good Food') also presents blancmange in the form of a chicken dish:

If you want to make a blancmange

This is how one should make a blancmange. Prepare some goat's milk and half a pound of almonds. Grind a quarter of a pound of rice to flour and dissolve this in the milk. Add a chicken breast that has been plucked, skinned and minced, plus a quarter of a pound of fat. Simmer in the milk for just as long as it takes to cook the chicken, then remove the pan from the heat. Now take a few ground violets and add them to the meat and milk, together with quarter of a pound of sugar. Serve straight away. During Lent, this same way of preparing a blancmange can be used to cook fish such as pike.

In the cuisine of the Renaissance, too, as represented by Martino da Como in his *Libro de Arte Coquinaria* (c. 1465) the classic blancmange recipe remains one for poultry.

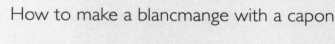

How to make a blancmange with a capon

In order to make 12 portions, take 2 pounds of almonds and grind them finely. To ensure that they remain as white as possible, let them soften in cold water for a day and a night before processing. Put the almonds in a pestle and mortar and when they are ground down, add a splash of cold water so that they do not lose their oil. Now take a capon breast and grind it with the almonds, along with some white bread that has been softened in a light stock made from the capon carcass. Mash this into the other ingredients. Now take a little verjuice and half an ounce of ginger that has been carefully peeled so that it is white. Add to this at least half a pound of sugar and thin the mixture with a little of the light capon stock. Rub this all through a fine sieve into a clean pot. Place this on a hot fire, but away from direct flame. Stir frequently with a spoon and let the mixture simmer for a good half hour. When the cooking time is up, add three ounces of rosewater. Serve the blancmange in bowls. Alternatively, use this mix to cover a whole roasted capon and then serve. If you want to make the blancmange dish appear even more refined, garnish generously with slices of apple before serving. And if you want to offer this dish in a two-coloured variety, first take an egg yolk and some saffron and mix these into a portion of the sauce. Add extra verjuice to this sauce to give it a sharper taste than the plain white version. Served in this way, the sauce may be described as having a golden-brown hue. If you have two capons, you can prepare one white sauce and the other yellow-brown.

The meat disappeared from blancmange by the 19th century at the latest. The use of meat in desserts has also largely disappeared in the Middle East. One exception is an Iranian dish, *khoresh mast*, which can nowadays only be found in Isfahan. This is a combination of yoghurt, honey, saffron and pieces of best end neck of lamb that have been sliced thinly before being boiled and then finely minced.

Rosewater

Middle Eastern ingredients which have long enjoyed great popularity in the West include various products made from roses – first and foremost rosewater, a floral essence obtained from the petals of the fragrant blooms. As in its region of origin, it was also regarded in the Christian West as a prestigious spice because of the high price it commanded and was only used very sparingly, mostly in desserts and occasionally on meat dishes. The recipe for its manufacture was a closely guarded secret; accordingly, in Middle Eastern cookbooks one only finds veiled allusions to how it was produced. It was a very different story, however, where medieval Arabic works on the natural sciences are concerned. Authors like the Baghdad doctor Ibn Jazla (d. 1100), for example, gave a very precise account of how it was made and the pieces of apparatus that were needed, in his book on dietetics that is known in its 13th-century Latin translation as *Liber de Ferailis et Condimentis* ('Book of Game and Condiments'). European cookbooks of the Middle Ages and the Renaissance likewise have very little to say about the production of rosewater.

One of the earliest mentions in England of rosewater as a cooking ingredient can be found in a recipe from a cookbook written during the reign of Elizabeth I, *The Proper Newe Book of Cookerye* (c. 1557). The recipe's name derives from the eggs' supposed resemblance to moons after being poached in a rosewater and sugar mixture:

To make egges in moneshyne

Take a dyshe of rosewater and a dyshe full of suger, and set them upon a chaffyng dysh, and let them boyle, than take the yolkes of 8 or 9 egges newe layde and putte them therto everyone from other, and so lette them harden a lyttle, and so after this maner serve them forthe and cast a lyttle synamon and sugar upon them.

Traces of Middle Eastern cuisine in British food

It may come as something of a surprise to learn that 'exotic' ingredients of Middle Eastern origin were not only known about but also incorporated into British cooking from as early as the Tudor period. Another, slightly later, recipe for 'sweet potatoes in rose and orange syrup' in *Elinor Fettiplace's Receipt Book*, written in 1605 during the reign of the first Stuart monarch James I, also involves rosewater.

Yet after the West's initial encounter with Middle Eastern ingredients, stimulated first by returnees from the Crusades and then by the growth of maritime trade, over the succeeding two centuries this culinary cosmopolitanism appears to wane. Surprisingly, by the 19th century, in an age that had seen Britain vastly expand its global empire, 'exotic' ingredients are conspicuous by their absence, even in cookbooks containing recipes of expressly Middle Eastern provenance. For example, the expanded edition of Eliza Acton's renowned *Modern Cookery for Private Families*, which was published in 1855, included a new chapter on 'Foreign and Jewish Cookery'. Here, we find two 'pilaws'. The seasoning of the Syrian version involves nothing other than salt and pepper, while the 'Simple Turkish or Arabian Pilaw (From Mr Lane, the Oriental Traveller)' is embellished by having '…a fowl, boiled almost to rags, […] laid upon the top' – though even here the writer maintains that 'the Turks and the Arabs generally add nothing to the rice but the butter, and salt, and pepper.'

A simple Syrian pilaw

This recipe was included in a chapter that was added in the 1855 edition of Eliza Acton's highly successful *Modern Cookery for Private Families*, originally published in 1845.

Drop gradually into three pints of boiling water one pint of rice which has been shaken in a cullender to free it from the dust and then well wiped in a soft clean cloth. The boiling should not be checked by the addition of the rice, which if well managed will require no stirring, and which will entirely absorb the water. It should be placed above the fire where the heat will reach it equally from below; and it should boil gently that the grain may become quite tender and dry. When it is so, and the surface is full of holes, pour in two or three ounces of clarified butter, or merely add some, cut up small; throw in a seasoning of salt and white pepper, or cayenne; stir the whole up well and serve it immediately. An onion, when the flavour is liked, may be boiled in the water, which should afterwards be strained, before the rice is added; there should be three pints of it when the grain is dropped in. Small fried sausages or sausage-cakes may be served with it at pleasure for English eaters. The rice may be well washed and thoroughly dried in a cloth when time will permit.

The tenor of the Victorian era is encapsulated in an even more famous cookbook of the period, Mrs Beeton's *Book of Household Management* (1860). In her recipe for Indian 'Mango Chetney' (*sic*), the author finds it necessary to explain to her readers her inclusion of garlic, an ingredient which 'was in greater repute with our ancestors than it is with our selves, although it is still used as a seasoning herb...the smell of the plant is generally considered offensive and it is the most acrimonious in its taste of the whole of the alliaceous tribe.'

Despite the old adage of travel broadening the mind, it seems on occasion only to have reinforced stereotypes regarding the inherent unpleasantness of foreign food. The explorer Charles Montagu Doughty, who journeyed around the Middle East, moving from Damascus to the *hajj* in Mecca in 1876–1878, and who later gave an account of his experiences in *Travels in Arabia Deserta* (1888), notoriously described Arab food as 'lambs sitting on mountains of rice in a sea of fat'.

The growth in popularity of Middle Eastern food in Britain

By the early 20th century, however, this parochial British attitude toward unfamiliar ingredients and foreign food was beginning to change. In their 1921 book, *The Gentle Art of Cookery*, Hilda Leyel (founder of the Society of Herbalists and the Culpeper chain of herbalist shops) and Olga Hartley attempted to revive a taste for the exotic, in chapters with titles such as 'The Alchemist's Cupboard' and 'Dishes from the Arabian Nights'. Here, the reader finds such recipes as *cherbah* ('An Arabian Soup very much eaten in the bazaars of Algeria and Tunis'), *oeufs à la Constantinopolitaine* and *imām bayıldı* (given here as *imaru bayeldi*).

The age of austerity that ensued in Europe in the aftermath of the Second World War, including the sheer lack of the necessary ingredients, left people with neither the time nor the opportunity to rediscover and explore the various forms of Middle Eastern cuisine. In the introduction to her 1999 cookbook *Tamarind & Saffron: Favourite Recipes from the Middle East*, the celebrated food writer Claudia Roden (who was born and brought up in Cairo in a Jewish household) recounts: 'When I first came to England in the mid-fifties, no one here had eaten aubergines, let alone cooked them. I had to explain courgettes as "baby marrows". You could only buy products such as pitta bread, filo pastry and vine leaves in Cypriot stores in Camden Town. Certain products such as sumac, the ground red berry with a lemony flavour, tamarind paste and the sweet and sour pomegranate syrup or molasses made from the boiled-down juice of sour pomegranates were not available anywhere.'

Yet this situation gradually changed in the 1950s and 1960s, notably with the publication of Elizabeth David's *A Book of Mediterranean Food* in 1950. This seminal work incorporated not only recipes from the South of France, Italy and Greece but also the Eastern Mediterranean (David had spent 6 years in Alexandria and Cairo working for the Admiralty and the British Ministry of Information during the war). Middle Eastern dishes in this work include *hummus bi tahina* and *ta'amia* – a *mezze* dish made of white beans – and even 'Turkish Stuffing for a Whole Roast Sheep'. In her wake came Claudia Roden, whose first publication *A Book of Middle Eastern Food* (1968) was the first work in English to deal exclusively with the cuisine of the region. She compiled the book from recipes given to her by other exiled Middle Easterners like herself.

Indeed, exile has been the driving force behind the exponential growth of interest in and availability of food from this region from the mid-20th century right up to the present day, as successive waves of refugees and migrants from the whole of the Near and Middle East have found themselves forced by conflict or economic necessity to leave their homelands and resettle in Western Europe and beyond. These range from the *Pieds Noirs* and others displaced by France's colonial conflict in Algeria in 1954–62 seeking refuge in the mother country, through the Turkish *Gastarbeiter* invited by the German government to come and work in heavy industry in the 1960s and 1970s to pick up the labour shortfall experienced during the country's period of rapid post-war growth (the so-called *Wirtschaftswunder*, or 'economic miracle'), to the more recent waves of refugees fleeing the devastating civil war in Syria that began in 2011.

These migrations saw the opening by migrants in the host countries of many food outlets, restaurants and takeaways, catering initially to compatriots but subsequently to increasing numbers of customers from the indigenous population. The sheer number of North African eateries in Paris and provincial French cities has led to talk of '*la conquête de la France par le couscous*'. Turkish and Balkan Muslim restaurants abound in Germany. At the top end of this market are Middle Eastern restaurants, notably run by former citizens of Lebanon ('the pearl of the Arab kitchen'), offering an extremely sophisticated dining experience. But the greatest success story throughout Europe has been at the other end of the spectrum: the spread of fast-food outlets producing readily edible street food conveniently wrapped in pittas or *khobez*, such as doner kebabs (*shāwarmā*) and falafels.

The term 'doner' derives from the Turkish word *dönmek* ('to turn'), which refers to the turning action of the vertical spit on which the stacked slices of meat (predominantly lamb) is grilled. According to some accounts, the dish is supposed to have originated in around 1830 in the city of Kastamonu in the Pontus Mountains; others place its genesis in Bursa in the 1860s. Certainly, the practice of grilling meat on a rotating spit had long been widespread throughout the Ottoman Empire. It is still predominantly sold as street food in Turkey. Originally the doner was a dish served on a plate and accompanied with rice and a mixed salad. According to an Arab cookbook of the 1990s, the meat for the spit is prepared in the following way:

Shāwarmā

The name of this dish, identical to the doner kebab, is an Arabised form of the Turkish *çevirme*, another word for 'turning'.

Cut 2 kilograms of lamb or veal (entrecôte or sirloin) into round slices of roughly 10 centimetres diameter. Tenderise these in the same way as you would a steak. Place the flattened pieces of meat in a glass bowl and add an onion sliced thinly into rounds, along with 5 grams freshly ground black pepper, 30 grams white pepper, a twist of grated nutmeg, a bay leaf, a few thyme leaves, half a cup of vinegar, chopped flat-leaf parsley and chopped green peppermint. Slice 400 grams of lamb fat into thin rounds and marinate them separately from the meat. Just before boiling (*sic*) the meat, add 30 grams salt to the water so that it cannot impair the flavour of the meat by drawing the juices out of it and leaving it dry. Marinate the meat for 24 hours. Now take a long spit of the kind that is specially designed for *shāwarmā* and use it to skewer the meat slices one after the other. After every three or four pieces of meat, impale a piece of fat, until the whole thing takes on a cone-like form. Mount the spit in an appropriate rotisserie fuelled either by charcoal or gas. The spit is constantly rotated to and fro. When the meat is done, slice off thin slivers using a long, sharp carving knife.

It is easy to see why this dish does not appear in current cookbooks of regional cuisine. Few people are willing or able to buy for their private kitchens the expensive rotisserie apparatus that is required, and which is only really worthwhile for commercial use. The success of the doner kebab through Western (and now even some parts of Eastern) Europe has to do with the particular way in which it is served. Even in the Lebanese cookbook from which the recipe above comes, one serving suggestion is to place the sliced meat inside a halved Arab flatbread, cut crosswise so that it forms a pocket. It was customary to garnish the *shāwarmā* meat with a few leaves of parsley or peppermint.

Commercial outlets now commonly serve the meat with a mixed shredded salad and a choice of sauces. A regular doner industry has meanwhile evolved around this popular food, supplying the fast-food outlets not only with ready-made doner spits but also the rotisserie equipment and all the other necessary accoutrements of a snack bar. The annual turnover of this industry in Europe is estimated to be greater than that of all other fast-food providers put together.

The increased demand for vegetarian food, especially among the young who are the principal consumers of fast food, has also seen the rise in popularity of another food of Middle Eastern origin that is ideally suited for the takeaway market and for quick consumption – the falafel (properly *falāfil*, which is related to the Arabic word for pepper). These small vegetarian rissoles are known as *ta'miyya* in Egypt; in this case, the word relates to the Arabic term for 'food' or 'foodstuff' (*ta'miyya* literally means 'light meal'). Originally the dish had in all probability been a Lenten fasting food for Eastern Orthodox Christians, i.e. the Copts in Egypt. There are two different ways of preparing them. In Lebanon, Syria and Palestine the principal ingredient is chickpea flour, whereas along the Nile this is replaced by white broad beans (*Ful nabed*) or brown fava beans (*Ful medames*). The chickpea variant is the one most commonly found is Middle Eastern restaurants in Europe. The recipe given by the Lebanese celebrity chef Ramzi Choueiri is perhaps the most elegant example of this simple but much-loved dish:

Falafel

Rinse and drain 400 grams dried chickpeas and 400 grams dried broad beans and leave them to soak in cold water for at least 8 hours overnight. Drain them in a sieve and then, using a food processor or hand blender, mash them to a paste with 2 finely chopped onions, 3 finely chopped cloves of garlic and 1 tablespoon finely chopped green chilli. Season the mixture to taste with salt, 30 grams freshly chopped leaf coriander, cumin, cinnamon and ground sumac. Leave to rest for 2 hours for all the flavours to blend in. Then take walnut-sized piece of the mix, roll them between your palms into little balls, coat them in white sesame seeds and shallow-fry them in groundnut or sunflower oil until golden brown on all sides; you may like to flatten them slightly before coating and frying to make turning them easier. Serve with warm flatbread and a salad of chopped tomatoes, spring onions, mint and garden salad leaves. If desired, the falafels can also be eaten with a simple sesame sauce (*tarator bi tahina*), made by mixing together tahini, lemon juice, water, salt and garlic to a runny consistency.

Preparation of this popular snack in commercial outlets is pure craftsmanship. The only way of ensuring consistency in the size of falafel balls is to use a falafel scoop when measuring out the paste. Middle Eastern housewives have also taken to using such implements. The fascination of this simple dish surely lies in its varied texture. On the one hand, the falafel has a quite heavy crust, formed in the frying process, and on the other a soft, almost mushy consistency inside. This tactile structure is in accordance with a Middle Eastern culinary ideal. Like doner kebabs, falafels are commonly served in a pocket of halved Arab flatbread in takeaway outlets in Western Europe.

Sweets

Above all, Middle Eastern sweetmeats have always been the kind of food that most stimulated the taste buds of consumers in the West. However, because of the often complex nature of their preparation, the great majority of these recipes were the domain of professional cooks and pastry chefs. In addition, they were long regarded as prohibitively costly. For at one time not only sugar but also almonds, pistachios and rosewater were expensive ingredients beyond most people's means. The following recipe comes from the cookbook of Philippine Welser, who as the first wife of the Habsburg ruler Ferdinand II, Archduke of Austria (r. 1564–1595), was easily able to afford such lavish ingredients.

Almond tart

If you want to make an almond tart, first put one pound of almonds on a table and grind or pound them and when they start to release their oil, add some rosewater. Once you have ground the nuts finely, put them in a bowl and add the whites of 5 eggs, cream and some more rosewater until the mixture is liquid enough to flow, yet without becoming too thin and runny. Spread this over the base of a tart tin that you have lined with pastry and blind-baked, then bake the filled tart carefully in the oven until just set. Towards the end of the baking time, beat together one egg yolk and rosewater and brush this over the set filling and the top and sides of the pastry to form a glaze. Return to the oven and bake for another five minutes or so.

Middle Eastern restaurants, groceries and specialist pastry shops, both in their home countries and in Western Europe, offer a range of desserts and especially pastries. These include *basbousa*, a semolina cake soaked in sugar syrup and variously flavoured with vanilla, coconut, lemon, or almonds; *ma'amoul*, pastries stuffed with either chopped dates or nuts; *konafa* (known as *kadaif* in Turkey), another pastry drenched in sugar syrup, made with a special (shop-bought) dough that looks rather like uncooked shredded wheat or vermicelli pasta, and filled with soft cheese; and the Moroccan pastry speciality called *m'hencha* ('snake'), so named for its resemblance to a coiled serpent, which is filled with a ground almond paste, or frangipane. In Middle Eastern countries, puddings and pastries such as these are always for serving with coffee or tea, or to mark special occasions such as Easter and Muslim festivals. Everyday meals invariably finish with fresh fruit rather than made desserts.

The common denominator of most Middle Eastern sweets and pastries is their undeniable sweetness, though this modern Iraqi dessert uses neither sugar nor honey as a sweetener, relying instead solely on the natural sweetness of the dates:

Madgūga

The name of this recipe actually means 'ground in a mortar'. Dried dates are recommended for this dish. *Medjool* dates are the finest, but other varieties such as *Deglet noor* are less expensive and work just as well.

In a heavy-based pan on the hob, heat 125 grams plain flour over medium heat until it begins to turn brown and give off an aroma. Remove from the heat and, in a processor or using a hand blender, mix 400 grams stoned dates and 3 tablespoons tahini with the toasted flour until you can form a ball out of it. If the mixture is too stiff, add a little more of the sesame paste. Now take 1 teaspoon each of ground cardamom, ground cinnamon and ground coriander seed and work them into the dough. Form little balls from the date mixture and press into each of them a roasted half-walnut. Roll the balls in sesame seeds and serve.

Consumers in the Middle East buy what is undoubtedly the region's most famous sweet – *baklava* – principally in specialist shops. That is understandable when one considers how time-consuming the manufacture of this dessert is. Even leaving aside the time needed to produce the pastry, which has to be left to rest for several short spells and then overnight, the whole process can take 2 to 3 hours. Even just making the pastry is hard labour. It needs to be repeatedly kneaded, and when it is finally stretched and rolled out, it must be so thin that you can see the back of your hand clearly through it. Nowadays, if people make *baklava* at home at all, they tend to buy in ready-made sheets of filo pastry, fresh or deep-frozen. In addition to this, the ingredients of *baklava* are nuts (walnuts, pistachios or almonds are favoured depending on the particular region), sugar, butter, nutmeg, cinnamon, and finally a generous helping of sugar syrup, flavoured with orange-flower water or rosewater. The labour-intensive nature of making *baklava* is probably the reason why recipes for it are not found in modern Arab cookbooks.

Today, the commercial manufacturers of *baklava* and other sweets are even more restrained in their use of sugar and honey than in the 1960s. In doing so, they are falling in line with a recent health trend observable in several Middle Eastern countries, which regards sugar as unhealthy.

Old and New — Modern Middle Eastern Cuisine

Practical and technical innovations in households large and small

From the first half of the 19th century on, Middle Eastern societies found themselves confronted by a European civilisation that was alien to them in many respects. Technological and medical innovations, and modern forms of literature or entertainment were imported to this region. However, it took some considerable time before modern kitchen equipment and methods of preparing food found their way into the kitchens of Middle Eastern societies. Admittedly, certain ingredients that were commonplace in Europe were processed in court kitchens in the palaces of regional and local rulers whenever the need arose to entertain European guests. But apart from that, people remained wedded to traditional dishes and cooking methods. In contrast to technological and medical advances, people were adamant that Eastern cuisine was superior to that of the West. Yet the preparation of traditional Middle Eastern dishes was extremely time-consuming. As long as there was an adequate supply of kitchen helpers to hand, there was little reason to engage with technically modern forms of European cooking practice.

Eating at table

The first thing to change was the way in which dishes were consumed. For centuries, people in the Middle East had eaten meals served on a sheet of leather or cloth spread out on the floor, or arranged on a large metal platter that was likewise placed on the ground or supported by a low metal frame.

You ate with your right hand, using as a rule your thumb, index finger and middle finger. Runnier dishes were eaten with a spoon. Pieces of flatbread could be used to help scoop up food. Among nomads, but also in many traditional private households and restaurants, it was perfectly possible to experience this style of dining until far into the 20th century, in places as far afield as Morocco and Pakistan. However, changes were afoot even as early as during the reign of the Ottoman sultan Mehmet II (r. 1808–1839). He preferred to eat in the European style at table and seated on a chair. The cutlery he used consisted of knives, forks and spoons, which were laid out in the Western manner. Mehmet was so fascinated by the European way of life that he even sent one of his cooks to Vienna to train as a chef. This cook, who went by the name of Hüseyin, worked from 1837 to 1839 in the kitchens of the Viennese royal court. We unfortunately do not know to what extent he was able to apply his new-found skills in the kitchens of the Topkapi Palace in Istanbul, since all the relevant cookbooks or other records have not been preserved. Certainly he would not have had much time or opportunity to give a practical demonstration of what he had learned to the Sultan, as Mehmet died in the year of his return.

Following the death of this forward-looking ruler, the Ottoman elite at first preferred to go on eating traditional dishes. But from the 1850s onwards, a section of the Ottoman ruling class began to take their meals at a table with chairs. The traditional method of dining continued to run in parallel with this, though the Hungarian traveller Hermann Vámbéry reported in 1870 that the upper echelons of the Ottoman Empire now ate at table. Two terms deriving from the Italian were coined to describe the different methods of dining: *alafranga* ('in the French style') and *alaturca* ('in the Turkish style'), which subsequently came to be applied to the dishes that were prepared. Yet it was not uncommon to find both kinds of dishes being served simultaneously.

In court kitchens and in those of the political elite, there was a host of different kitchen implements: every conceivable kind of cooking pot and pan, larger and smaller dishes as well as vessels so large that a whole lamb could be cooked in them. Traditional pots and pans were made from copper, whose tinplate coating constantly needed refreshing in order to prevent the copper from reacting chemically with the food and releasing harmful agents. Copper pots and pans were also in widespread use in urban households in the provinces of the Ottoman Empire. Depending on how wealthy a household was, expensive or cheap cooking utensils were used which varied not only in their quality but also in whether they were equipped with handles and lids. Another criterion was the number of pots and pans a family owned. Other kitchen implements were made of wood, including various trays, cutting boards, spoons, ladles, and rolling pins. Some pieces of equipment were also made of earthenware or glass, such as beakers and mugs and clay pots in which food items like vegetables for example could be simmered slowly. Baskets of many different sizes were shaped and woven from osiers and grasses. There were special cooks' knives and a variety of implements for cleaning the kitchen like brooms, soap dishes and so on. In large kitchens, the cooking area consisted of a series of interlinked clay ovens or stone-walled ovens. Bread was baked in these ovens, as well as various other dishes. In some regions of the Middle East like the city of Sana'a in Yemen, certain families even had baking ovens of three different sizes. The smallest was used primarily in the mornings, to avoid having to heat up the large oven to make flatbreads. In the kitchens of less well-off families it was the practice until well into the 20th century for unbaked loaves to be taken to a public baker to be finished in his oven. So that different people's breads did not get mixed up, they were imprinted with individual motifs. Even in the late 20th century, many kitchens still had braziers made out of sheet iron which stood on four legs.

Skewers of meat were grilled over the red-hot charcoal heated in the braziers, or alternatively aubergines and red peppers, which were then used as ingredients in other dishes after grilling. Generally speaking, this kind of equipment could also be bought at markets in Middle Eastern cities in the 19th century. If a family needed large cooking vessels for a major celebration like a circumcision or a wedding, they could rent them out for a small fee at the Blacksmiths' Market. From the 18th century onwards, an increasing number of manufactured goods from the European porcelain and glass industries came into use in the cities of the Middle East. For instance, from the first half of the 19th century, there was a family from Bohemia living in Baghdad who controlled the trade in kitchen glassware over several generations. And from the 18th century on, fine bone china pieces from the Meissen and Dresden porcelain manufactories in Saxony enjoyed enormous popularity among the elite classes of the Ottoman Empire.

For a long time, the supply of fuel posed a problem in several regions of the Middle East. Prices could fluctuate enormously between regions. During the reign of the Mamelukes in Egypt and the Levant between the 13th and 16th centuries, wood was very expensive in Damascus but by comparison astonishingly cheap in Beirut. The only area where coal was mined was the

Ferghana Valley in Central Asia and it was scarcely known in other areas. Consequently, wood and charcoal were the commonest fuels. Great importance was attached to fuels giving off as little smoke as possible when they were burned. Medieval Arab cookbooks recommend the woods of the palm tree, the holly and the olive as particularly suitable, while readers were discouraged from using fig wood on account of its propensity to produce a lot of smoke. The cookbooks also strongly advised against the burning of camel dung – a practice that was frequently referred to in the reports of European travellers to the region. Fires were kindled with twigs, hemp stalks and shards of chopped wood. In order to economise on precious fuel, people avoided building roaring fires and instead cooked dishes as slowly as possible.

Unfortunately, there is a dearth of studies on objects of daily use in Middle Eastern kitchens between the mid-18th century and the 1950s, or indeed on energy and water supplies during that same period. All that we do know is that water was for a long time drawn from public wells.

House owners who had a well on their property, along with the associated pumping systems, could count themselves very lucky. A public, centralised water supply only came into operation in Istanbul at the beginning of the 1940s. The situation was no different in Damascus and Baghdad, either. However, one may fairly assume that new kitchen utensils had begun to arrive in the Middle East from the start of the period of European colonisation. These would first and foremost have been pots and pans made of either cast iron or wrought iron, which had the advantage of not having to be constantly recoated like the old copper pans. As things stand, there is no evidence to indicate that the large cast-iron cooking ranges that became widespread in European kitchens from the 1850s onward were also imported into the Middle East.

Fundamental technological change only came about once it became possible, in the years after the Second World War, to fill metal cylinders with propane gas. Gas ovens and hobs that ran off propane could quickly reach high temperatures. At the same time, though, the temperature could easily be regulated. In addition, propane could be transported in cylinders and bottles of various sizes. Compact gas burners that can just accommodate a single pot are still widespread. Basically, this was a development of the situation that housewives in many working-class districts of Middle Eastern cities had found themselves facing since time immemorial: they only had a single source of heat at their disposal, which they used predominantly to produce stews.

On the other hand, larger gas cylinders could be used to fuel ovens and hobs with multiple rings of the kind that can still be found in the kitchens of the middle classes in cities of the region. Like the equivalent gas cookers in Europe, these ovens generally have three to four rings and an oven. The empty propane cylinders need to be changed regularly. Often, these heavy gas bottles are moved around on low, two-wheeled trolleys, which when empty generally become play equipment for the children of the neighbourhood. Lorries laden with gas bottles racing noisily around the narrow streets are a familiar sight in Middle Eastern cities.

In more upmarket kitchens, the gas ovens are customarily built into large tiled floor units which also provide space for storing bowls, plates and other kitchen equipment. In less well-appointed households, a solid masonry plinth normally provides a surface for individual gas rings or two- or three-burner hobs to stand on, connected to the gas bottles behind with flexible hoses.

Electric ovens are still very much the exception, a fact that undoubtedly has to do with the erratic electricity supply in many parts of the Middle East. Mains electricity was a long time coming to the region, only being introduced to Istanbul, for example, in the 1930s. This explains why refrigerators primarily ran on gas prior to the Second World War. Electric fridges began to gain a growing foothold in homes, grocery stores and restaurants in Turkey from the 1950s onwards. These were followed soon after by deep-freeze units, which first appeared in larger food shops. Presently, though, smaller freezer appliances also became available for home use and quickly found a ready market. Nowadays, there is a great demand for fridges and even freezer units installed in cars, especially in certain regions of the Arabian Peninsula, where there is a long tradition of picnics.

Modern preservation techniques

The technology of manufacturing food cans was developed in France and Great Britain at the beginning of the 19th century, and it was not long before tinned foods also found their way into Middle Eastern households. However, the most successful tinned foodstuff from Europe, meat extract, found no market among those of the Islamic faith. Devout Muslims were extremely sceptical as to whether this product obeyed the precepts of ritual purity. The same applied to corned beef. On the other hand, tomato purée was readily accepted, though the real hit among consumers was condensed milk, which right up to the 1980s could be found in the smallest shops in the Middle East. Yet canned goods remained too expensive for many consumers, which is no doubt why they came to be regarded in many cases as a premium product.

The increased production of deep freezes from the 1980s on prompted a series of fundamental changes in the international food market, which was also able to expand its range of deep-frozen goods to the countries of the Middle East. Even so, it took a while for manufacturers to take on board the special requirements of Middle Eastern societies. At the heart of the matter was the question of the ritual purity of the foodstuffs on offer. There was basically no problem where vegetables were concerned, or likewise fish and fish-based products, as long as it could be guaranteed that no alcohol of any kind was involved in the manufacturing process. Gelatine poses a particular problem for Muslims. It is avoided because it is usually made from pork derivatives. And in the matter of deep-frozen meat products, it had to be ensured that everything was *halāl*. Some groceries provide magnifying glasses so that shoppers can look at packaging and check the lists of ingredients and production methods.

As elsewhere in the world, deep-frozen foods represented a time-saving boon to Middle Eastern consumers. This was necessitated by the trend there, as in the West at the same time, toward a dwindling number of domestic servants in middle-class households. Yet this gain in time had one unexpected consequence. A sociological study conducted among families in Libya in the 1980s reported that women, principally from traditional households, complained of boredom after finding themselves with hardly anything to do around the house after the introduction of labour-saving devices and of semi-prepared food and ready meals. In the absence of their husbands, though, who were often working away from home, they couldn't leave the house. One of the few possibilities for variety in their lives was the recent introduction of home video players and tapes for rental. Conversely, however, women in more modern households now had the opportunity of taking paid employment and starting careers without neglecting the home.

Welcome technological innovations included pressure cookers, which made it possible to prepare dishes involving dried chickpeas or broad beans far more quickly than before. This means that it is no longer necessary to go through the laborious process of soaking and boiling pulses; for it is the case that Middle Eastern housewives still prefer to make dishes like hummus, say, from the ground up, believing shop-bought, ready-made products to be less tasty. In the 1980s, a Japanese firm developed a special appliance that made steaming rice a much simpler business. Traditional methods of preparing rice in Iran, for example, involve the absorption principle and can take from one and a half to two and a half hours. Using the Japanese quick rice steamer, Iranians can not only cook rice much more rapidly now, but even produce the crust on the base (*tahdig*) that is so highly prized.

Changes in gastronomy

Until far into the 19th century, the professional hospitality industry was not especially well developed, in either the Middle East or Europe. More sophisticated restaurants only came into existence in France after the French Revolution, spreading gradually thereafter across the rest of Europe. Certainly, prior to this, inns and taverns had existed where a person could stay the night after partaking of some simple fare. But these places had a bad reputation and were associated with prostitution and homosexuality. Restaurants frequented by people in search of a good or exceptional meal are a relatively new phenomenon. In the Middle East too, there had always been particular locations where travellers could stop and rest. In caravanserais, guests could store their goods securely and have their pack animals stabled, fed and watered. To cater for their own refreshment, travellers had to purchase ready-made food, drinking water and fruit juices at the local bazaar. Anyone who wanted to indulge in illicit drinking could do so in taverns on the outskirts of towns. These establishments offered not only wine and beer but also prostitutes, who freely plied their trade.

First restaurants

Restaurants in the European sense only began to appear in the Middle East in the late 1870s. They sprang up first in places visited by Western tourists taking the 'Grand Tour'. In the large cities of Egypt, Syria and Palestine, as well as in Istanbul, they catered to the requirements of European travellers. These establishments were often run by 'Levantines' – adherents of the Catholic faith who had been resident in these regions for generations, but who originally came from such places as Greece or Armenia. Several other of the hosts were people who had only recently emigrated from Europe and had fallen into this profession by chance. In the French colonies and spheres of influence in the Maghreb and the Levant the owners were Frenchmen who had often undergone professional training as restaurateurs. Apart from this, various Italians, Austrians and even a few Germans could be found in these positions.

The meals offered by the Levantines were largely based on Middle Eastern models. In winter, pork was even served. The restaurateurs and hoteliers who came from Europe initially served dishes from their countries of origin. In particular, Italian cuisine with its many and varied pasta dishes, found favour with the indigenous middle classes and was for instance adopted into the cookery canon of Egyptian families, often in combination with a hollandaise sauce. Until the 1980s, such dishes were regarded as chic, even though in terms of quality they were not a patch on home-grown cuisine. In *A Book of Middle Eastern Food* (1968) the author and food historian Claudia Roden recounted how well-off Egyptian families would give their servants small sums in cash so that they could buy food for themselves. The servants would then cook their own food up on the flat roof terraces of the luxury blocks of flats, where their quarters were situated. 'Sometimes all the servants of one block pooled their purchases or money to make one large, communal dish. The strong aromas enveloped the street below, drowning the limper, delicate perfumes of their masters' refined dishes. The rich defended themselves from the accusation that they ate well while their servants had only cheap food by saying that the latter *preferred* their own food. There was a great deal of truth in this, and I know many children of rich families who would sneak up to the roof terraces to share their servants' soups and stews.' It is in this context that Claudia Roden gave the recipe for a special lentil soup.

Spinach and lentil soup

Put 250 grams large brown lentils, cleaned and washed, in a large saucepan. Cover them with about 2 litres water, bring to the boil and simmer for 20 to 40 minutes until they soften. Meanwhile, defrost 250 grams frozen leaf spinach in a colander. Cut into pieces or ribbons. Fry 1 large, finely chopped onion to a russet colour in 2–3 tablespoons of oil. Add the prepared spinach and sauté over a low heat. It will release a considerable amount of juice. Let it stew in this liquor, covered, for a few minutes, then pour into the pan with the cooked lentils. Stir in 2 tablespoons tomato concentrate, season to taste with salt and a pinch of cayenne pepper, and simmer until the flavours and colours have blended. Add a little more water if the soup is too thick, season to your liking, and serve.

Modern restaurants

In the main centres of international tourism like Istanbul, Cairo, Aswan, Jerusalem and various places in North Africa such as Marrakesh, luxury hotels of a very high standard arose, where for the most part a French-inspired *haute cuisine* was served, of the kind that was to be found at similar high-end establishments around the globe. A prime example of this was the Mena House Hotel near the Great Pyramids of Giza, which first opened its doors in 1885, at first on a seasonal basis, and from 1890 received guests the whole year round.

These belonged primarily to the business and political elites of the Middle East, and to international High Society. Members of the Egyptian or Ottoman elites were extremely discerning guests, who could afford to spend the hot summers at popular tourist resorts in the south of France or Switzerland. After the Second World War, it was fashionable among wealthy North Africans, Egyptians, or Lebanese to take a plane to dine in Paris or Rome and afterwards fly back home. On other occasions, though, this same clientele was extremely partial to the various dishes of their own native cuisines. From the 1950s onwards, with the changes in the kinds of jobs people did and the hours they worked, and particularly their increasing tendency to be employed away from home, many small, unpretentious restaurants sprang up in the centres of the larger metropolises of the Middle East, offering a limited choice of well-known traditional dishes. Their décor consists, even to the present day, of simple tables and chairs. The crockery and cutlery are of similarly low quality. Water is provided free of charge in glass carafes. Alcoholic drinks are not served, but there are plenty of soft drinks on offer. There is generally no menu, but instead the waiter tells customers what the dishes of the day are. An instant decision is called for, and the dishes, prepared in advance and kept warm, are brought to table without delay. A typical dish one might encounter in these eateries is *musaqqaʻa*.

Musaqqaʻa

Finely dice 2 medium onions and 2 cloves of garlic; sweat these in olive oil until soft. Add 500 grams sliced aubergine and cook until they are almost falling apart. Pour in a can of sieved tomatoes and briefly bring to a simmer. Add salt and finally a quantity of pre-cooked chickpeas. The dish is served with plain rice or flatbread.

There are numerous variations on this basic recipe, though the key ingredient always remains aubergine. *Musaqqaʻa* can be served as an accompaniment to grilled meat but is often served simply as a vegetarian main dish.

The prices are geared to the services offered. At the end of the meal, a glass of sweetened tea is served. Although the *chaichi* (tea vendors) work in the restaurants, they do so off their own bat, and pay the restaurant owners a small sum for the right to peddle their wares in the premises. This kind of restaurant has no pretensions to high culinary quality, nor is this expected by their exclusively male clientele. Some traditional restaurants boast a somewhat more refined décor, but basically offer the same bill of fare. Several of them have a separate area designated the 'family section'; in some countries this is located on the first floor. Here, women are permitted to dine in the company of male relatives. The habitués of these restaurants are mostly members of traditional families who are travelling on business or civil service assignments and who have no relatives in the vicinity to entertain them. Generally speaking, these establishments are seen as something of a stopgap measure by their clientele. Because of the large distances between their home and their place of work and the notoriously congested streets of large Middle Eastern cities, men cannot practically go home for lunch. Come what may, women tend to take the view that they can cook better and above all far more economically at home; accordingly, they regard eating in such restaurants as foolish and wasteful.

Since the 1990s, a number of alternatives to these basic restaurants have opened in the so-called 'Shopping Malls'. A wide range of businesses offer their wares for sale in these multi-storey buildings, which can be seen as the modern equivalent of bazaars. Among the shops are various fast-food restaurants belonging to international chains such as McDonald's or Kentucky Fried Chicken. To a certain extent, these outlets have in the interim fallen in line with local tastes by including, alongside their regular fare, some Middle Eastern starters and classic light main dishes on the menu. As alternatives to the multinationals, a few local or regional chains have also sprung up, offering a wide array of Middle Eastern dishes that can be consumed on the go. During Ramadan, these outlets provide special menus, and include corresponding pointers to their Islamic character. These restaurants usually have a section where customers can sit down at tables and benches; air-conditioning makes for a pleasant temperature. Consequently, during the month of fasting and on the Thursday before Friday prayers, the malls are frequented by crowds of people, predominantly from the poor quarters of the cities, who find the air-conditioning a real luxury. They spend their time window-shopping, amazed at the goods on offer and the prices charged. Young people find the malls an ideal place to socialise, and a visit to a fast-food restaurant counts among the highlights of these trips.

The period since the 1960s has also seen the growth in the major cities of the Middle East of upmarket cafés and restaurants that do not have any special, regionally restricted fare on their menus. One can order dishes like simply grilled fish with a side and a salad, for example, and finish the meal with a choice between fresh fruit and a crème brûlée. These establishments are favoured by businessmen, politicians and army officers as places where they can have confidential discussions. Alongside these, a number of extremely high-end restaurants have also emerged, offering a sophisticated take on Middle Eastern cuisine served in elaborate, consciously oriental interiors consisting of wooden panelling with traditional inlay work, indoor fountains and seating arrangements comprising low, cushioned settles and short-legged tables. The waiters are dressed in appropriate garb: embroidered shirts, waistcoats and harem pants. Live oriental music is also played. One of the recipes commonly found in such restaurants in Beirut is 'Chicken with yoghurt' or 'Assyrian chicken':

Dajaj suryānī (Assyrian chicken)

Divide a good quality, free-range chicken (weighing 1 kilogram) into eight portions, place them in a casserole or tagine with 1 large peeled and finely diced onion and 2 crushed garlic cloves, cover with cold water, bring to the boil and simmer gently, with a lid on, for 20 minutes. At the end of the cooking time, lift out the chicken pieces and retain the broth. Mix the chicken with 2 tablespoons flaked almonds, 125 millilitres of the chicken broth, salt and pepper. Meanwhile, in the oven, lightly bake 2 flatbreads until they turn crisp and remove. Now set the oven at a low setting (150°C/ gas mark 2) and bake the chicken and almond mixture until lightly browned. To serve, break the flatbreads into small pieces and distribute them across four plates and then pile the chicken pieces on top, two per person. Finish with 2 spoonfuls of plain yoghurt on top of the chicken mixture, sprinkled with a little sumac.

This recipe is a reconstruction of a dish served at the al-Wazir restaurant in Beirut in the early 1970s. The name of the dish refers to the Assyrian (or Syriac) Christian ethnic minority, who are spread across several countries of the Middle East, rather than to the ancient people of the same name.

Since the 1970s, all major hotels in the Middle East, irrespective of whether they belong to international chains or are owned by local entrepreneurs, generally have at least one restaurant devoted to the cuisine of the respective country. But because the taste preferences of their European and American guests are paramount, the dishes served in hotel restaurants do not accord with the culinary expectations of their Middle Eastern clientele. If the latter don't want to eat traditional food, they will deliberately choose to dine in those hotel restaurants offering French or Italian cuisine. Even in the international hotels, cooks must nowadays adhere strictly to Muslim dietary requirements. Particularly where the ban on using alcohol is concerned. Plus, pork is never found on the menus.

Over the past decade, a form of fusion cuisine has grown up between Morocco and the Arabian Peninsula. Ideas and techniques from the most diverse traditions are being adopted and developed further. The internet is playing a major role as a conduit of information in this regard.

In view of the multifarious possibilities presented by fusion cuisine, some Middle Eastern commentators have started to question what will become of individual culinary traditions. They point to the healthiness of traditional cooking and the relative cheapness of its ingredients. They frequently cite the experiences of European kitchens in absorbing the many influences of foreign culinary traditions, applaud current trends in those cuisines towards returning to local and regional ingredients and preparation methods, and earnestly hope for similar moves in their own food culture.

Your Food — Our Food: The Role of Politics and Economics

Politics and economics

The British call the Germans 'Krauts' and the French 'Frogs' by way of poking fun at these nationalities' predilection for sauerkraut and frogs' legs respectively. During the Second World War, the United States changed the term 'Sauerkraut' to 'Liberty kraut' – a move that found an echo several decades later during the US and British invasion of Iraq in 2003 (which France refused to support in the absence of a United Nations resolution), when 'French fries' were briefly rechristened 'Liberty fries'. Germans use the derogatory term 'Spaghettis' for their Italian fellow Europeans, while in 2010 the German minister for family affairs expressed her outrage on learning that children 'from migrant backgrounds' were calling their 'indigenous German' classmates 'Spuds' *(Kartoffeln)*. These are just a few examples of the fact that the foods which foreigners like or eat a lot of are often used as a label to characterise or caricature them. Conversely, eating habits and traditions contribute to the formation of a people's or region's own identity. For instance, for many centuries polenta (cornmeal, made by milling maize into a flour) constituted the staple diet of poor people in the north of Italy, where it formed the basis of both savoury and to a lesser extent sweet dishes. Even though poverty no longer drives its consumption, many northern Italians are still very partial to polenta and prefer it to pasta. So strongly is it associated with this region that southern Italians disparagingly refer to their northern compatriots as *polentoni* ('polenta eaters').

Culinary identities

In the Middle East, likewise, national identity is determined by culinary traditions. The German Islamic scholar Anke Bentzin describes this phenomenon in her account of her field research among Uzbek immigrants in

Istanbul, and quotes one of the women she interviewed: 'Take my mother-in-law, for instance. I have a Turkish sister-in-law. She invited us all round to her house for dinner. We turned up, and my talented sister-in-law had prepared no fewer than eight separate dishes. She'd really made an effort, serving up some extremely elaborate Turkish dishes plus some of our Uzbek cuisine as well. But there was no *pilav* [an Uzbek rice dish]. Whereupon my mother-in-law promptly announced: "This isn't dinner! She hasn't cooked us any dinner at all!"' As far as the old Uzbek woman was concerned, *pilav* was an indispensable element of an Uzbek meal, no matter what else was being served up. Cultural and political identities thus evolve, among other routes, via culinary customs.

Dolma in Iraq

In the mid-1960s the Iraqi English-language newspaper *Baghdad News* conducted a survey among the wives of accredited foreign ambassadors resident in the capital about the impressions they had formed of their host country. As befitted diplomatic protocol, the ladies who were questioned gave uniformly friendly and positive responses about Iraq and its inhabitants. When asked what their favourite Iraqi dish was, to a woman they all, regardless of their nationality, replied: dolma. In giving this answer, they were echoing a view prevalent among Iraqi housewives, both at that time and still nowadays, that 'stuffed vine leaves' are a particularly refined Iraqi national dish, and hence ideal for serving to guests. Yet the name *dolma* is of Turkish origin and the dish is commonly found far beyond the borders of Iraq. *Dolma* comes from the Turkish verb *dolmak*, meaning 'to fill'. The word has been assimilated not only into Iraqi Arabic, but also into Albanian, Armenian, Azeri (the language spoken in Azerbaijan), Greek, and Farsi (Persian). Dolma customarily denotes vine leaves stuffed with various mixtures of meat or rice. The same recipe is also found in Syria, Lebanon, Palestine and Egypt under the name *waraq 'inab*.

In countries of the Caucasus, on the other hand, the variant *dolmeh* is used.

Dolma

Prepare and cook 100 grams long-grain (basmati) rice in the usual way. Sweat 2 finely chopped onions and 2 crushed cloves of garlic in olive oil until translucent and then add 250 grams minced beef or lamb; cook on a medium heat and stir constantly until the meat is nicely browned all over. Add the rice, flat-leaf parsley, dill or mint, 3 tablespoons lemon juice, a half teaspoon of ground turmeric, a pinch of dried oregano, salt and pepper and continue cooking for another 5 minutes, stirring all the time. Now take the pan off the heat and set aside. In a clean frying pan, briefly dry roast 50 grams pine kernels, but on no account let them burn. Add these to the minced meat mixture. Meanwhile, blanch 40 pickled vine leaves in boiling water for a minute before tipping them immediately into a bowl of cold water; carefully separate the leaves and dry them on sheets of laid-out kitchen paper. Line the base of a heavy-bottomed dish with a single layer of leaves, then take the remaining 30 or so vine leaves and use them to make little packages filled with the meat and rice mix. Place these close together on the bed of leaves in the dish and sprinkle with 2 tablespoons olive oil and a little water. Bake in the oven at a high heat for ten minutes or so, then reduce the temperature to around 180°C/gas mark 4, cover the dish tightly with foil and allow them to steam for 50 minutes. At the end of cooking uncover the dish and allow the dolmas to cool to room temperature before serving.

The classic filling for dolma is meat with rice and pine nuts, but an alternative is to make them vegetarian. As is the case with many traditional dishes, there are numerous variations.

The fact that dolma is seen as the Iraqi national dish shows how difficult culinary attributions can be, even on political grounds. In spite of its Turkish name and the dish being a familiar feature of many cuisines across the Middle East, neither the Turks nor the Lebanese, nor indeed the Syrians or the Palestinians claim it as their national dish. The Iraqi cookbook author and historian Nawal Nasrallah has pointed out that the practice of stuffing vegetables was common in Mesopotamia even at the time of the Abbasids. But even she is at a loss to explain why, out of the all many dishes that were devised during the Middle Ages, dolma in particular should have attained the status of the national dish of Iraq.

The dispute over hummus and falafel

The current Middle East conflict over the 'Holy Land' (Israel/Palestine), which began with the establishment of a League of Nations mandated territory in the region in 1920 after the dissolution of the Ottoman Empire, is even played out in the kitchens of the region. Ideologists and practitioners of Zionism, whose aim it was to establish a national state for the Jewish people, were convinced that a nation should also have a national cuisine or at least needed one or two characteristic national dishes. The idea was that immigrants to the new Jewish state, who came from many different countries and various culinary traditions, would thereby be reminded that they all formed part of a single nation. Zionism, which at least during the phase of the foundation of the state of Israel in 1948 had a socialist flavour, chose as the Israeli national dishes two simple Middle Eastern recipes that all the new state's citizens could afford: hummus and falafel. As early as 1940, the Hebrew daily newspaper *Haaretz* explained how to prepare falafel. The Zionists conveniently chose to forget that both dishes had a long Arab background, in much the same way as the cultivation of oranges was heralded as a genuine Israeli achievement. Of course, in doing so a certain amount of historical back-story had to be created for both dishes. In the spirit of an 'invented tradition,' therefore, allusions to chickpea dishes were 'discovered' in the Torah, which were then used to corroborate a supposed Jewish tradition of eating such food.

The popularity of hummus and falafel among Muslim and Christian Arabs on the one hand and Jews on the other undoubtedly has to do with them being purely vegetarian dishes, which means that no awkward religious dietary problems can arise in eating them or offering them to others. As early as the 1960s, Arab commentators like the Syrian sociologist and connoisseur of Arab cuisine Sadiq al-Azm (1934–2016) complained that the adoption of hummus and falafel into the Israeli national culinary canon represented a kind of cultural appropriation: 'They haven't simply taken away our lands. Now they are depriving us of our cuisine as well.' Indeed, in that same decade the Israeli embassy in Washington, DC, distributed a cookbook entitled *Beyond Milk and Honey*, in which for example falafel was described as an Israeli dish. And back in the 1950s a song about falafel which ran as follows did the rounds in Israel: 'Once, when a Jew came to Israel, he'd kiss the ground and give thanks to his Maker. Now he's scarcely stepped off the plane before he's buying falafel.'

The divergence of opinion over the national affiliation of hummus and falafel turned into a fierce competition from 2006 onwards. As a stunt to try and increase their turnover, the Israeli food manufacturer Sabra Food established a record for inclusion in the Guinness Book of Records in March of that year by producing a huge tub of hummus 3.5 metres in diameter. The propagandistic splash this created led to the launch of a rival record attempt in Lebanon, which ended with a portion of 1,350 kilograms of hummus being made. The attempt was accompanied by the slogan 'Hummus is Lebanese'. Ultimately, in January 2010, a group of hundreds of cooks in the Arab village of Abu Gosh 10 kilometres west of Jerusalem on Highway 1 prepared a hummus portion weighing a massive 4,000 kilos, which in the absence of any other receptacle large enough to contain it was served in a satellite dish measuring six metres across. This particular Arab village is renowned for its restaurants and above all for the quality of its hummus. Together with a neighbouring Israeli village, it also fielded a joint Arab-Israeli football team. The organiser of the enterprise, Jaudat Ibrahim, commented: 'I'm pleased that we've been able to shift the focus of the Middle East conflict through hummus. It's better to argue over food than to clash over other matters. I'm saying to the people in Lebanon, Syria, Jordan and Egypt: I know the situation is difficult, because there's no peace. But I'd really like it one day if we could make a dish with ten tons of hummus in it. Then we could set about sharing it with the whole of the Middle East.' And indeed, some Lebanese cooks duly produced a humous weighing 10,452 kilograms. Sadly, though, it did not lead to any improvement in relations between Israel and its Arab neighbours.

Israeli and Arab firms turn out hummus as a finished product, which they then sell on the American and European markets. Of course, housewives in both the Arab states and Israel maintain that freshly prepared hummus is the only thing to eat and that the mass-produced item could never even come close to rivalling the quality of a hummus made at home. In practice, however, industrially manufactured hummus has a large customer base both at home and abroad. A further twist in the 'Hummus Wars' is the attempt by Lebanese producers to get the European Union to accord it Protected Geographical Status as a quintessentially Lebanese foodstuff. If this bid succeeds, it would mean that hummus made by Israeli food concerns could not be marketed any more under that name in Europe. The dispute involving the food designation authorities of the EU is still ongoing.

Unlike hummus, falafel is a product that should, wherever possible, be eaten freshly made. In the Middle East and Europe alike, it is generally offered for sale at small snack bars. In Israel, you can buy postcards showing falafel balls with little *Magen David* ('Star of David') national flags stuck in them. Falafel is regularly handed round at official receptions hosted by Israeli state institutions, and this has contributed to it losing its reputation somewhat in the country as cheap and simple fare. Falafel too has witnessed the rise of a processed variant. In this case, the dried ingredients are sold as a ready mix to which the consumer just needs to add water before shaping and frying the falafel balls.

But such products have been largely shunned by housewives and food outlets and their clientele, and it has not thus far grown into a major market. A Falafel War is therefore not on the cards.

Chefs for Peace

In addition to the initiative undertaken by Jaudat Ibrahim in Abu Gosh, mention should also be made of the organisation 'Chefs for Peace'. This body was set up in November 2001 in Jerusalem by a native son of the city, the Armenian chef and entrepreneur Kevork Alemian. Ten years prior to this, he had met two chefs, one of them Jewish and the other an Arab Muslim, at a conference of the Slow Food movement in Italy. Working together in a kitchen on a daily basis had given them an insight into each other's culture, and so it was decided to set up a non-profit organisation with the aim of fostering understanding on a culinary level between members of the different religious communities within the city of Jerusalem. At the time of writing, nine Christian, Jewish and Muslim head chefs of restaurants are involved in 'Chefs for Peace'. They organise events of various kinds, including communal dinners in different restaurants, primarily in Jerusalem and Israel, but also in European cities. Members of 'Chefs for Peace' also conduct guided walking tours, informing participants about the culinary situation in Jerusalem.

It is to be hoped that the parties in conflict concentrate less on trying to outdo one another in terms of quantity, as in the Hummus Wars, and more on collaborating to develop basic recipes. As an example of this, we might cite a new take on falafel devised by the British restaurateur Silvena Rowe, who is of mixed Bulgarian-Turkish heritage:

Crunchy red Swiss chard falafel

Heat 1 tablespoon of olive oil and sauté 1 red onion, 2 teaspoons ground cumin and ¼ teaspoon ground allspice in it for 3-4 minutes. Set aside in a bowl. Fill a large saucepan with water and bring to the boil. Drop in 500 grams Swiss chard and blanch for 2 minutes. Drain immediately and, once they're cool enough to handle, squeeze the leaves dry. In a medium non-stick pan, bring 220 millilitres milk to the boil then reduce to a simmer. Little by little, whisk in 100 grams chickpea flour until you have a smooth paste. Keep the mixture moving to avoid lumps. Then season, add 3 more tablespoons of olive oil and cook on a low heat for 8 minutes, stirring all the time with a wooden spoon. Like choux pastry, the mixture will come away from the sides of the pan and work into a ball, solidifying as it is heated. Cool the ball of paste, then mix in the sautéed onions, 3 tablespoons cooked chickpeas, 3 tablespoons of lemon juice and the blanched chard. Using your hands, mould the mixture into small balls and arrange on a tray. Chill in the fridge for a couple of hours. In a pan, heat until very hot enough oil to cover the falafel balls. Carefully place the falafel into the oil and cook for 3-4 minutes, until golden brown. Remove with a slotted spoon and place on kitchen paper to drain.

With this recipe, from her renowned 2010 cookbook *Purple Citrus & Sweet Perfume*, Silvena Rowe suggests serving a tahini, sumac and lemon sauce:

Mix 3 tablespoons tahini with 1 teaspoon ground cumin and the juice of two small lemons in a bowl. Slowly stir in 1–2 tablespoons water, a little at a time, until you have the consistency that resembles double cream. Then add the garlic, and season. Combine ½ teaspoon crushed or ground sumac with 2 tablespoons olive oil and drizzle over the sauce, Sprinkle with 1 teaspoon black cumin seeds and serve.

Other conflicts over the origins of foods

A similar culinary clash recently took place on the island of Cyprus, which is divided between Greeks and Turks. Before the enforced partition of the island by a Turkish military invasion in 1974, production of the cheese *halloumi*, or *hellim* in Turkish, was widespread among both populations. This semi-hard cheese was generally accepted as a common Cypriot national product. Greek and Turkish producers cooperated both in its manufacture and in its marketing. But from 2015 on, voices on the Greek side began to claim ever more insistently that it was a Greek Cypriot product and that, as such, it should be granted Protected Geographical Status by the European Union. The Turkish *hellim* producers on the island were up in arms at this suggestion, fearing that any such ruling would restrict them to selling their product exclusively in Turkey, and possibly Lebanon as well. The fact that cultural historians ascertained that this sheep and goat's milk cheese had even been made in Ancient Egypt did not make the situation any simpler.

A similar controversy surrounds the question of the origin of stuffed vine leaves (dolma). A German newspaper recently reported on a dispute between Armenia and Azerbaijan regarding this. Since the fall of the Soviet Union in 1991, a bitter enmity has existed between the two countries, in which Azerbaijan has accused Armenia of committing genocide, among other things. The newspaper discovered that this hostility even extended to culinary matters: 'In Azerbaijan, entire television programmes are devoted to demonstrating that Armenia has no national dish of its own… And exactly the same thing happens in Armenia.'

According to the website Epochtimes Europa there is a question of who invented the famous Middle Eastern dessert *kanafeh* (also known as *kunāfa*). On the website, French academic Mathilde Chèvre, an Arabist at the *Institut français du Proche Orient* (French Institute for Near Eastern Studies) describes how to prepare the pastry for these crèpes, which are filled with a mixture of ground almonds, sugar, cinnamon and orange juice and drenched in a syrup made from lemon juice, sugar and grated orange peel, but at the same time maintains that the process is so time-consuming that one would be better off buying it ready-made from an Arab delicatessen. In July 2009, a world record was set in the Palestinian town on Nablus in the West Bank for producing the largest portion of *kanafeh* ever made, weighing 1,765 kilograms and measuring some 74 metres in length. Once cooked, it was shared out among the spectators. A statement issued by the organisers of the event maintained that its purpose was to present Palestine in a more positive light. Yet at the same time, it was also about proclaiming *kanafeh* as a Palestinian dish and countering claims that it originated in Egypt. In addition, one further intention may have been to preempt any potential attempts on the part of the Jewish state to co-opt *kanafeh* as an Israeli dish, just as it had done with hummus.

New forms of gardening

The phenomenon known as 'urban gardening' that has attracted an increasing number of followers in the major cities of the West in recent years has long been a characteristic feature of the metropolises of the Middle East. This kind of private gardening is widespread in Cairo, for example. This metropolis and its surrounding suburbs are home to an estimated 20 million people. Moreover, the population is rapidly increasing due to high birth rates and a steady influx of people from the country coming to the city to seek work. Among the many challenges associated with this kind of demographic situation is the difficulty of providing such a vast number of people with sufficient food, and moreover food that is healthy. Inevitably, shortages are a recurrent problem. It is the ordinary Egyptian housewives, many of whom come from the countryside, who are attempting to alleviate the situation by growing their own food on small urban plots. In many cases, the families of these women live in multistorey buildings crammed close together in the poor quarters of the city. For years, some families have been keeping chickens and even sheep on the flat roofs of these tenement buildings. The 'ruralisation' of Cairo, which is a regular topic of discussion in sociological studies, therefore manifests itself not only in the social sphere but also in quite practical economic activities. For some years now, women have also been cultivating small vegetable gardens on these flat roofs, in the form of raised beds.

Here, they grow herbs like rosemary, mint, parsley and basil, along with various salad crops, tomatoes or bell peppers. For the most part, the raised beds are mounted on table-height supports and have porous bases so that any excess water can drain through; there is an ingenious arrangement underneath that collects the water so that it can be reused. The produce grown is often so abundant that the women are able to supplement their meagre housekeeping money by selling a portion on to greengrocers' shops in the neighbourhood. Men are involved in these urban gardening projects only in vanishingly small numbers. By contrast, even before moving to the big city, women were heavily involved in running traditional smallholding enterprises in their home villages in the Nile Delta or Valley.

Halāl as an economic factor

In the first decade of the 21st century, according to a report by the Sinologist Madlen Mähus, student refectories were set up at many Chinese universities, where meals were prepared according to the prescriptions of Sharia law. The Beijing authorities made aggressive propagandistic capital out of this special dietary provision. For although the number of Muslims living in the People's Republic – 27 million – is greater than that of countries like Tunisia, Syria, or Saudi Arabia, the fact that they still make up only 2 percent of the entire Chinese population means that they nonetheless represent a tiny minority. This makes it all the more remarkable that meals served in mass canteens should be prepared according to *halāl* requirements. The general perception of *halāl* dishes as particularly healthy may play a role. In addition, vegetarian dishes are often more popular among Muslims. These may well have been decisive factors in gaining acceptance for this move among an academic non-Muslim public in China. Above all, however, major manufacturers of Islamic food who operate globally offer a wide range of finished products and so-called 'convenience' meals that are very attractive to operators of large canteens for serving to their clientele.

The country from which most products of the Muslim food-manufacturing industry are exported worldwide is Malaysia. Firms there even send goods to China, which in 2007 provided investment capital to the tune of US $500 million to help set up a 'Malaysia International Halal Park'. First and foremost, though, the Malaysian food industry exports its goods to neighbouring Indonesia, the Indian Subcontinent, the Middle East, and Muslim minorities resident in European countries, especially in Great Britain. The systematic organisation of Muslim food production in Malaysia was the focus of a state-subsidised and controlled initiative from 1981 onwards, under the administration of Prime Minister Mahathir Mohamad. Responsibility for monitoring compliance with Muslim dietary regulations was vested in the Department of Islamic Development Malaysia from 1982 on, which issued the relevant *halāl* certifications against payment of an officially set fee. The Department of Islamic Development issues these certifications not only for home-produced goods but also confirms the compatibility with Islamic prescriptions for goods from the non-Islamic world. Thus, there is a *halāl* certificate for Coca-Cola or for various foodstuffs made by the Swiss manufacturer

Nestlé. The authorities frequently criticise the fact that in Europe, private bodies or private individuals are responsible for issuing *halāl* certifications for food, notwithstanding that many of these organisations have patently lacked the necessary expertise for making such weighty judgements, such as the Islamic Food and Nutrition Council of America and the Islamic Co-ordinating Council of Victoria, Australia. Competition is therefore not confined to the economically enormously important market for the production of *halāl* foodstuffs but also extends to the business of issuing *halāl* certifications. A statement given in 2006 by the Australian Federation of Islamic Councils makes clear exactly which markets are involved both now and in the future in an international context. The c. 1.4 billion Muslims in the world live to a great extent in regions where the food they eat has to be imported. Many of these countries have the highest per-capita incomes in the world and the fastest-growing middle classes.

At the same time, these societies also have the highest birth rates globally. In future, therefore, the demand for pure, properly accredited Muslim foodstuffs and for *halāl* certifications is set to rise steeply.

The people responsible for organising the marketing of *halāl* products also identify in the worldwide interest shown by Muslims an opportunity to initiate a kind of Muslim free-trade zone. Nor would the goods traded in this zone be restricted to foodstuffs, but would also include cosmetics, dental products like toothpaste, pharmaceuticals, clothing, and specialised Muslim banking products, insurance policies and educational offers. All these goods and services also require *halāl* certification. The advocates of this kind of Islamic free-trade zone take the view that the worldwide criticism currently being levelled at Islam and the growing mood of Islamophobia following the events of 11 September 2001 have prepared the ground for such an economic entity. For as a result of the negative attitude toward Islam, even many Muslims who are not so strict in the observance of their faith are increasingly turning to the consumption of *halāl* products. The enormous market power these consumers represent has in the interim become clear to even the most important non-Muslim players in international trade.

Over and above the narrow economic aspects, the Malaysian government also sees state support for the products of the Muslim food manufacturing industry as a means of showcasing the country as cutting-edge, progressive and Islamic in a very modern, forward-looking way. In doing so, it also identifies a possibility of proclaiming the kind of moderate Islam practised in Malaysia. By introducing an identifiable logo for *halāl* products, Malaysia has clearly managed to impose its standards on the international Muslim market for food in a lasting way.

On the occasion of the opening of the Malaysia International Halal Showcase in 2004, the country's then prime minister Abdullah Ahmad Badawi stated this aspiration unequivocally when he said: 'Today we will mark the unveiling of a new standard for Malaysia – a Muslim standard for the world.'

His statement was referring specifically to the launch of the Malaysian Standard MS 1500 under the auspices of the country's Department of Standards. This encompassed general regulations for the preparation, handling and storage of *halāl* products. An additional aim of these stipulations was to facilitate and improve cooperation with food manufacturers operating within a global market.

A Southeast Asian chicken dish showing influences both from India and from the Middle East, is a prime example of a *halāl* recipe from the Indonesia/Malaysia region:

Nasi kebuli

In a heavy-based pot, heat 3 tablespoons butter or oil over a medium heat, and then add 10 peeled and finely chopped shallots, 7 peeled and finely chopped or crushed cloves of garlic, a small knob of minced or grated root ginger, 1 teaspoon ground coriander, 1 level teaspoon white peppercorns, a twist of nutmeg, a small piece of stick cinnamon, 4 crushed green cardamom pods, 2 cloves, a stem of crushed lemongrass, a small piece of galangal, half a teaspoon of shrimp paste *(blachan)* and a splash or two of soy sauce. Briefly fry these ingredients together until the aromas start to rise. Then add to the pan 500 grams of chicken (breast or thigh meat, to taste) skinned and deboned and diced into small cubes and turn up the heat to high until all the pieces are browned. Deglaze the pan using 250 millilitres chicken stock (fresh or made up from a prepared stockpot or cube), add a pinch of salt and simmer gently until the chicken is fully cooked. At the end of cooking remove the chicken pieces with a slotted spoon, and set them aside, keeping them warm. Now tip 250 grams long-grain (basmati) rice into a clean, lidded wide-based frying or sauté pan with another 250 millilitres chicken stock and bring to the boil. Reduce the heat, cover the pan and simmer until the rice is almost fully cooked through. Add the chicken and keep cooking until the rice is completely cooked and no longer chalky. Bring to table in a wide serving bowl garnished with some more lightly browned shallots and 250 grams fresh pineapple, cut into small cubes.

❧ ❧ ❧ ❧ ❧ ❧ ❧ ❧ ❧ ❧ ❧ ❧ ❧ ❧ ❧ ❧ ❧ ❧

New *halāl* concepts

Over the last two decades or so, some new concepts of Muslim life – including dietary dictates – have kept on emerging among Islamic communities resident in the USA and Canada. A good illustrative example of this is the Taqwa Eco-Food Cooperative in Chicago. The Arabic word *taqwā* can be translated as 'fear of God' or 'mindfulness of God', and refers to the Muslim lifestyle taken in its totality. The Taqwa Eco-Food Cooperative therefore uses as a matter of principle only those foodstuffs that are in accordance with the injunction to 'preserve the Divine Creation'. So, where meat is concerned, not only does the cooperative observe the rules regarding ritual slaughter, but also requires that the animals are kept humanely, that the producers receive a fair price, and that all those who are involved in rearing and slaughtering the animals and in processing their meat are paid a decent wage. The representatives of the *taqwā* thus supplement the concept of *halāl* with that of *zabīh*, a term that derives from the Arabic word *dhabīh*, and which can be roughly rendered as 'correctly slaughtered'. In this context, the literature produced by American organisations affiliated to the *taqwā* movement often talks in terms of 'sustainable' and 'sustainability'. This focus on sustainability concerns not just meat but also extends to all provisions.

According to *taqwā*, Muslims should try wherever possible to buy local and regional products and to ensure that ecological principles were taken into consideration in their production. It is not Islamic legal scholars or imams who are promoting this way of life but rather lay people with a highly personal interpretation of the authoritative texts of Islam. But they do refer frequently to works by the Iranian-born scholar Seyyed Hossein Nasr (b. 1933). Now living in the USA, Nasr is Professor Emeritus of Islamic Studies at George Washington University in Washington, DC. Another influential figure in the Muslim ecological discourse is Ibrahim Abdul-Matin, whose 2010 book, *Green Deen: What Islam Teaches about Protecting the Planet*, has made him one of the most important spokespersons of the Muslim ecological movement in the USA.

In the UK, the Muslim population currently numbers some 2.8 million, or around 5 percent of the total; this figure is set to increase to around 8 percent – or 5.6 million – by 2030. This represents a sizeable market of predominantly meat-eating consumers (especially lamb; it is estimated that British Muslims eat around one-fifth of all the lamb sent to slaughter in the country). And it is the question of *halāl* slaughtering methods which forms one of the main ethical animal welfare issues facing Muslim consumers in the UK. Specifically, the debate turns on whether the animal is stunned prior to having its throat slit in accordance with the precepts of Islamic law. As it stands, some 88 percent of all *halāl* meat comes from animals that have been stunned, but the remaining 12 percent continues to be the subject of controversy even within the Muslim community (leaving aside the country at large, where this issue has been exploited by certain right-wing newspapers and pressure groups to stir up Islamophobia). Of the country's two foremost *halāl* certification boards, the Halal Food Authority permits stunning, while the Halal Monitoring Committee bans it. Perhaps the ultimate solution will lie with demographic shifts, as a growing Muslim middle class – whose members, just like their non-Muslim compatriots of the same class, care about the quality of their food and the conditions in which it was produced – demands high animal welfare standards across the board and is prepared to pay a premium to guarantee them. And indeed, there are far broader issues at stake than just stunning, which have to do with Islam's emphasis on sustainability and kindness to animals. As Muhammad Nazir, CEO of the *halāl* food producer Ghanim International UK, maintains: '*Halāl* is so much wider than just how an animal is killed or about meat. It's about eating food that benefits an individual in their physical and spiritual wellbeing.'

The *halāl* food market in the UK is worth over £1 billion and all of the major supermarkets now stock a range of lines suitable for the Muslim consumer. There is now an annual London Halal Food Festival, inaugurated in 2013 and held at Tobacco Dock in the East End, which in 2017 attracted some 18,000 visitors over a weekend to the stalls of over 100 exhibitors. Another indicator of the growing popularity of *halāl* is the launch of an online *halāl* supermarket delivery website, Maalgaari, which serves the whole of central London.

Foodstuffs among strictly conservative Muslims in the diaspora

The question of the ritual purity of food is of paramount concern above all to conservative neo-Salafist groups in Europe. According to the French Islamic scholar, Olivier Roy: 'Of course, neo-fundamentalists have no interest in the art of cooking or cuisine. Everything that is *halāl* is good, making ingredients and recipes completely irrelevant.' Correspondingly, they also have no interest in the various culinary traditions of the Near and Middle East. Instead they perceive the differences between these cuisines as a sign of the insufficient unity of the Islamic community, which in their view needs to be rectified. Because ritual purity is at the front and centre of their assessment of foods, neo-Salafists have no problem in consuming fast food that is on sale in the countries where they reside. Their key concern is not with any culinary tradition or any special tastes, but with a ritual norm. Regardless of whether it is burgers or falafel, the key question is the food's ritual purity. They can even drink Coca-Cola, although there has been an attempt in France to establish an alternative brand 'Mecca Cola' for the Muslim market. As regards food, the fundamentalists are less sensitive than they are in matter of dress, where at least in western Europe they cleave to a set of 'invented traditions' such as the *shalwar* (baggy trousers) and *kameez* (long shirt), which form the national dress of Pakistan but are garments which were completely unknown to the contemporaries of the Prophet Muhammad. By contrast, in the view of neo-Salafists, foodstuffs remain ethical and neutral in religious terms just as long as they can deemed to be *halāl*. Thus, in their eyes, the market in food is not a religious but a global one.

Conclusion

Eating and drinking in the family circle or with friends, hospitality, rituals and feast days have been central themes in the literature of the Middle East since time immemorial; whether in pre-Islamic Arabic poetry, the Qur'an or the Traditions of the Prophet *(ahadīth)*. Many culinary examples can be found in the extensive collections of Arab, Persian or Turkish proverbs. The literary scholar Sabry Hafez once set himself the task of determining the percentage of sayings that were devoted to food or drink in the respective collections. He discovered that some twenty percent of all the proverbs cited related to eating or drinking! These include general proverbial observations like 'Eating a lot doesn't make you strong', or 'If you eat everything today, what will you have tomorrow?'. But there are also a number of sayings that refer to specific food items or ingredients, for example: 'If you find a meal with fruit outside the gate of an orchard, then don't go in', or 'Anyone who figures on getting his neighbour's gravy will go without supper that evening'. In the modern literature of various Middle Eastern countries, too, there are a host of culinary references such as 'Bread and Salt' for a collection of short stories or 'Olives and Dates'. Oranges frequently appear in the titles of books, as in the famous novel *Ard al-burtuqal al-hazin* ('The Land of Sad Oranges') by the Palestinian writer Ghassan Kanafani (1936–1972).

Ingredients and meals are innocuous topics of conversation among men, allowing interlocutors to skirt thorny issues like political debates or religious quarrels. Rather, people can relax and compare notes on what they think about a new restaurant or discuss the dishes that were served the last time Ramadan fasting was broken. For women, they provide an opportunity to boast of their domestic skills. On the other hand, oblique criticism of the political circumstances or the socioeconomic situation of a country can be skilfully woven into discussions that are ostensibly about food or drink, as in the simple anecdote: 'Two men are standing on one of the peaks of Mount Qasioun (Jabal Qasioun) overlooking Damascus. One says: "All those chimneys down there are factories!", to which the other replies: "No, they're kitchens!"' A simple-minded informant of the ubiquitous Syrian secret service would be hard put to see in this an attack on the ruling regime. And yet this is exactly the manner in which people in such repressive societies formulate a veiled criticism of prevailing political or social conditions.

A lively interest in culinary themes in Middle Eastern societies is also attributable to the fact that the ready availability of food, we might even say superabundance of food, to which we have become accustomed in recent decades in several Western societies, does not form part of most people's experience in the majority of Middle Eastern societies. Time and again, the historical records tell of famines triggered by armed conflict or climatic catastrophe. In AD 639, for example, a famine is said to have swept the whole Arabian Peninsula under the reign of the second caliph 'Umar ibn al-Khattab (r. 634–644). Often, however, a lack of wheat as a staple foodstuff was a problem restricted to a particular region. According to an account by the Arab universal historian al Mas'udi (896–956), in Baghdad in 814, under conflict conditions that were threatening to become a full-scale civil war, bread in the west of the city was twenty times the price of the same commodity in the east. The reason for this was that the west was encircled by an impregnable ring of troops laying siege to it, whereas the rest of the city could be provisioned without any difficulty. In Egypt, a series of failed harvests between 1064 and 1072 cost more than 10,000 people their lives. Periodically the port city of Alexandria found itself immune to these ravages, since it could be supplied with grain by ships from Greece. When the Central Asian ruler Timur (d.1405) was forced to retreat from Asia Minor, his withdrawal sparked a famine in the region.

And finally, a shortage of basic provisions was reputed to be one of the factors behind the popular uprising in 2011 against the Syrian leader Bashar al-Assad.

Even access to clean drinking water is not a given in many regions of the Middle East. Water often has to be carried over long distances from a well. As a general rule, transporting the heavy clay pots full of water always has been, and still remains, a task for women. Right up until modern times, carriers went around the major cities dispensing water from large leather panniers. Some of them would sell cool water to thirsty passers-by. Mains water piped into houses and flats is an amenity that only arrived in the late 19th or early to mid-20th centuries.

Many households in Middle Eastern societies were and still are dependent to a great extent on fluctuating international food markets and, where staple foodstuffs are concerned, on local harvest yields. This situation has promoted a lively exchange of information between people about techniques for preserving food and the best ways of preparing special, less common ingredients. In Morocco, *khlii* is a typical way of preserving meat. This involves cutting beef into long strips, salting them heavily and leaving them to marinate for a whole day, wrapped in linen sacks as protection against vermin. It is then rubbed with spices, salt and fat and marinated for a further 24 hours. At the end of this period, it is put back into linen sacks and hung up in the sun to dry, a process that can take several days. The sacks have to be brought into the house at night to prevent the meat from being exposed to overnight moisture and the morning dew. When the meat is completely dry, it is cooked in a mixture of oil and water before it is sealed in preserving jars. This dish can be found on the menu in many Moroccan restaurants. If a customer orders it, however, the waiters are often keen to find excuses as to why they cannot serve it. They claim it is either too greasy for the time of year, that it hasn't been stored for long enough yet, or that it needs to be pre-ordered. This makes it a favourite topic of conversation among friends. Recollecting tasty or uncommon dishes provides a way, especially in times of austerity, of overcoming present hardships while at the same time holding out hope of better times ahead.

Humorous anecdotes about eating and drinking, poems and naturally the art of cookery itself are common themes for table talk, as well as for long cross-country journeys by taxi or on one of the many bus lines between the region's major cities. Competitions often arise over who can recite the most texts. Short poems are particularly popular:

We live among beasts,
Who wander around looking for new pastures
But have no wish to increase their understanding.
In their eyes, he who writes on fish and vegetables
Has superior merit;
While he who teaches true science
Is tiresome and boring.
(Salih Ibn 'Abd al Quddus, died 738)

The sun, moon and stars
Like being reflected in the river's water.
Then the sun becomes a loaf and the stars eggs
And the full moon a buffalo-milk cheese in the pond.
(Ibn Sudun, died 1464)

A favourite disputation turns on the question of where a particular dish was created or which chef is especially adept at making it. Poems such as the ones above are all part of the Middle Eastern tradition of oral communication. The sharing of dishes from one's travel provisions on cross-country journeys and on numerous other occasions helps forge or intensify personal relationships. Both verbal and concrete culinary exchanges, however, are not conducted consciously to this end. These form an integral part of the cultural traditions of the Middle East and are learnt and passed down from childhood as a positive, ethical mode of behaviour. Despite the moderation that Islam exhorts its followers to observe, even in acts of generosity to all and sundry, it has always proved impossible to hold this fundamental attitude of sharing in check.

In the UK, one of the most remarkable culinary success stories of recent years has been the growth of the small chain of high-end restaurants and delicatessens in London owned and run by the chefs Yotam Ottolenghi and Sami Tamimi. The two men were born in Jerusalem in the same year, 1968, a few miles from one another but on opposite sides of the Israeli–Palestinian divide; Ottolenghi is an Israeli Jew, and Tamimi an Israeli Arab. However, they only met in the late 1990s when both came to London to work in the catering industry. Together, in 2002, they opened a delicatessen in Notting Hill, West London, with Tamimi making savoury dishes and Ottolenghi pastries and sweets, which soon gained a loyal following thanks to the chefs' unconventional flavour combinations and their prominent use of vegetables. Yet the keynote of their refreshing style of cooking was and still is the tastes of their Middle Eastern homeland, with ingredients such as (home-made) harissa, the Palestinian spice blend *za'atar*, rosewater, and pomegranate molasses much in evidence. The profile of the brand was further raised not only by the opening of further outlets across the capital but also by Ottolenghi's authorship of a weekly column for *The Guardian* newspaper from 2006 onwards, entitled 'The New Vegetarian' (though he is not in fact a vegetarian) and, jointly with Tamimi, a series of acclaimed cookbooks, including *Ottolenghi: The Cookbook* (2008) and *Jerusalem* (2012). In 2014, the *London Evening Standard* remarked that Ottolenghi had 'radically rewritten the way Londoners cook and eat'.

On the credit side, the story of Ottolenghi and Tamimi points up the many commonalities that link people of different religious and ethnic backgrounds in the Middle East, one of the prime examples of this being a shared culinary heritage. Their fruitful and friendly collaboration lends a lie to the lazy popular assumption that there exists some innate animosity between Arabs and Jews. And their inventive cuisine has made a major contribution towards raising the profile and status of Middle Eastern cuisine in the West, moving it away from its rather downmarket associations with doner kebab shops and falafel snack bars. But on the debit side, the fact that their collaboration first took root in London only serves to highlight the generally more bleak picture of a rapid decline of cultural (and culinary) symbiosis in the Middle East itself.

Over many centuries, Middle Eastern societies were multinational, multiethnic, multireligious and socially highly diverse; the Turkish Nobel laureate Orhan Pamuk's 2003 book, *Istanbul: Memories of a City*, for instance, shows the Turkish capital as a vibrant cultural melting-pot in the 1950s and 1960s. Existing national, ethnic, social or religious barriers were regularly and readily broken down above all by exchanges on a culinary level. But the second half of the 20th century and the early 21st have witnessed a rise of religious fundamentalisms and strident nationalisms in the region, a development exacerbated by the propensity of major global or regional powers – in the Cold War, the capitalist USA and the communist Soviet Union, and latterly Sunni Saudi Arabia and Shiite Iran – for fighting proxy wars in the region. In addition to an appalling loss of life, the result has been a deadening tendency towards monoculturalism. Sadly, culinary connections have managed to survive the political and religious upheavals and violent conflicts of the past quarter-century in only a few isolated places. We can only hope that in future, more peaceful times, these will swiftly re-establish themselves as part of a great and enduring common tradition.

Index of Recipes

Metric Conversions

1 gram is the equivalent of 0.035274 ounce (oz).
1 kilogram is the equivalent of 2.20462 pounds (lb).
1 millilitre is the equivalent of 0.033814 US fluid ounce (oz).
1 litre is the equivalent of 33.814 US fluid ounces (oz).

Glossary of Ingredients

Aloe A succulent flowering plant, aloe contains a very bitter juice that was once used as a flavouring. People are advised against using aloe as a cooking ingredient nowadays because of its laxative properties.

Ambergris Wax-like substance produced in the digestive tract of sperm whales. Greasy and with a sweet scent, it was used in the Middle Ages as a seasoning in the East, but also in the West both as a very expensive seasoning and restorative and in the manufacture of perfumes.

Bay leaf The leaf of the laurel tree, which can be used in cookery either fresh or dried. It imparts a warm flavour to dishes but should be removed before serving as it is unpalatable.

Betel nuts Unripe nuts of the Areca palm are sliced, mixed with calcium hydroxide (slaked lime) and wrapped in the leaves of the Betel pepper plant (*Piper betle*), from which the nuts incorrectly derive their common name. Because betel nuts are very bitter they are usually eaten together with peppermint or licorice. A mild intoxication results from slowly chewing the nuts, which have traditionally been taken as a stimulant to combat tiredness.

Camphor A substance derived from the resin and bark of the large, evergreen camphor laurel tree, which is found in Southeast Asia (particularly Indonesia). It has long been used for its scent in cooking and for medicinal purposes, and is mentioned as an ingredient in both savoury and sweet dishes in medieval Arabic cookbooks such as *Kitab al-Tabikh*, compiled by the 10th-century Baghdad writer Ibn Sayyar al-Warraq.

Cardamom A plant of the ginger family native to the Indian Subcontinent and Southeast Asia, cardamom is known particularly for its small, green seed pods. The resinous black seeds are ground and used in a variety of foodstuffs, principally sweets and beverages. Turkish and Lebanese coffee is often heavily flavoured with ground cardamom. A larger variety, Black (or Nepal) cardamom, is used mainly in savoury dishes.

Cassia, or **Chinese cinnamon**   Spice produced from the aromatic bark of East Asian evergreen trees, cassia has a taste like cinnamon, though less delicate. Much of the spice sold as cinnamon in the United States and Europe is in fact cassia; true ('Ceylon') cinnamon is far easier to grind to a powder than the thick, woody bark of cassia.

Chili, or **Cayenne Pepper**   Fruits of the genus *Capsicum*, native to Central and South America. Available in varying degrees of heat from greengrocers or spice markets, they are used in both their fresh and dried forms to lend heat to dishes.

Cinnamon   'True' cinnamon (*Cinnamomum verum*, see **Cassia**) is native to Sri Lanka, hence its alternative name of Ceylon cinnamon. It is used principally as a flavouring in sweet dishes such as the pastry *baklava*, but is also added in small quantities to North African tagines that combine meat and fruit.

Cloves   The aromatic flower buds of a tree (*Syzygium aromaticum*) native to the Molucca Islands ('Spice Islands') in Indonesia. Cloves were first brought to the West by Arab traders, and later cultivated on Mauritius and Zanzibar. They are used whole to season dishes, but should be removed before serving.

Coriander, or **Cilantro**   A robust herb and spice grown for culinary use, both for its fresh green leaves and its seeds (used whole or ground). The seeds are best crushed before use to release the maximum taste. Coriander is easy to cultivate.

Cumin (*Bunium persicum*)   A very popular spice in all Eastern cuisines, from a plant native to the Middle East and India. Its seeds are used in both whole and powdered form.

Curry powder   A typical spice mix used in Indian cuisine, consisting chiefly of turmeric, with smaller amounts of ground cumin, coriander seed and chili powder. The Curry tree (*Murraya koenigii*), which is native to India and Sri Lanka, is unrelated to curry powder. Its leaves, which smell of limes or mandarins, are also used in South Asian cooking.

Date syrup Available in healthfood stores and on the Internet, date syrup is obtained from stoned dates that have been simmered in boiling water and then filtered.

Dill A green herb that grows widely in Eurasia. In the East, the tips of the fine, thread-like leaves are used to flavour rice, fish, meat, vegetable and pulse dishes. Available fresh or dried, the plant is easy to grow.

Fennel Native to India, the bulbs of the fennel plant are eaten as a vegetable, while its fine feathery leaves and its seeds are used as spices. Fennel has a mildly aniseed taste.

Galangal A plant belonging to the ginger family, its roots are widely used in Southeast Asia for culinary seasoning and for medicinal purposes. Galangal is now increasingly available in the West in Asian supermarkets.

Garlic A species of Allium (onion) known for its especially pungent aroma. The bulb, with its fleshy cloves, is the most commonly used part of the plant.

Ghee A form of clarified butter widely used in Asian and Middle Eastern cuisines. The butter is clarified by being gently heated, while the water and scum that rise to the surface are skimmed off before the clear liquid fat that results is poured off and kept. The solid residue that sinks to the bottom is discarded. Ghee, which is high in saturated fats, can be heated to a higher temperature than butter in deep frying.

Ginger The large, fleshy rhizome of the ginger plant is a popular spice addition to many Eastern dishes (e.g. ground with garlic to form a paste base for a range of South Asian curries), and is also made into tea infusions. Ground, dried ginger is an ingredient in curry powders, while the candied stem of the ginger plant is commonly used in desserts.

Lemon grass, or **Citronella** Used primarily in Southeast Asian curries and fish dishes, lemon grass is the stalk of a perennial tropical Asian grass variety. To release its flavour, it must first be pounded or chopped and infused in a base liquid such as coconut milk but removed before serving as its woody, fibrous texture makes it inedible.

Mastic, or **Arabic Gum**   A resinous substance obtained from the mastic tree. It is a widely used spice in the Eastern Mediterranean, used in ice creams, sauces and seasonings. Mastic has a refreshing flavour reminiscent of pine needles or cedarwood.

Mint   A widespread herb available in many different varieties; the sweet variety spearmint is especially popular in the Middle East, and forms the basis of the green tea infusion called Moroccan mint tea. Its cool, refreshing flavour also makes it an ideal addition to salads such as the bulghur-wheat dish *tabbouleh*.

Musk   A secretion of the abdominal gland of the Musk deer, a species of Eastern and Central Asia, musk is a strong-smelling substance. It was formerly used in Middle Eastern kitchens, mixed with rosewater, to flavour pies and other dishes, but this practice has now died out, not least because of the endangered status of the deer species and the huge cost of musk (comparable to ambergris); it is now confined to use in perfumes.

Murri   A sour-tasting condiment thought to have been made from brine and fermented barley or fish (like the Ancient Roman *garum*) and used in Medieval Arabic cuisine.

Nutmeg   The seed of an evergreen tree that grows in the tropics (originally only on the Banda Islands in the 'Spice Islands' of Southeast Asia). It is used sparingly as a spice to flavour various dishes both savoury and sweet.

Pepper   A universally used condiment available in several different varieties. It was very expensive during the Middle Ages.

Pomegranate   Difficult to cultivate, the pomegranate is primarily used for culinary purposes in the form of juice or pomegranate molasses, a thick, sweet-sour syrup widespread in Middle Eastern and North African cuisine.

Prunelle A small, yellow, sharp variety of plum similar to the mirabelle, predominantly found in Southern Europe. Generally sold dried and without the skin.

Quince A stone fruit of the apple and pear family from which jams and juices are produced. After parboiling (the quince is very hard and dense), the flesh can also be added to meat dishes, such as Moroccan tagines. The Spanish fruit paste known as *membrillo*, commonly eaten with Manchego cheese, is made by boiling quinces vigorously with sugar.

Raisins Desiccated grapes, which need to be reflated in water before adding to sweet or savoury dishes. Raisins are available in several different varieties.

Rose petals/Rosewater The petals of scented roses can be used either fresh or candied as a garnish on sweets or meat dishes. Rosewater is a distillation of rose petals. Dried and crystallised rose petals may be purchased in Asian groceries, while rosewater is more widely available.

Rue The bitter-tasting leaves of rue were used in ancient Near Eastern and Roman cuisine as a culinary herb and in traditional medicines. It is not typically found in modern cooking.

Saffron The most expensive spice in the world, obtained from the dried orange-red stigmas of the saffron crocus flower. It has a unique sweetish aroma, which has been compared to the scent of musk or ambergris, and colours rice, potatoes and other vegetables it is cooked with in yellow.

Spikenard A flowering plant of the Valerian family, native to the Himalayas of Nepal. The oil obtained from it was used sparingly to season foods in Ancient Roman and medieval times, most particularly dishes involving white meat.

Sumac A mildly bitter, lemon-flavoured powder made from the dried fruits of one particular species of Sumac tree (*Rhus coriaria*). Because the fruits of other species of this tree are poisonous, the spice should only be bought from a reputable source.

Tahini Paste made from toasted sesame seeds that have been hulled and ground. It is widely used in Near Eastern cookery, notably as the basic ingredient for the confection *halva*.

Thyme Mediterranean herb that grows abundantly in the wild in the south of France and elsewhere. It is easily cultivated, and has a pleasant, earthy smell and taste.

Turmeric A plant of the ginger family, whose rhizomes are sold fresh or dried and which, when desiccated and ground, produces a bright yellow powder that is a key ingredient in many Middle Eastern and Asian dishes. The Moroccan spice mix *ras al-hanout* typically contains turmeric. Its vivid colour makes it ideal as a dye and for bulking out the more expensive and subtly flavoured saffron.

Verjuice (literally 'green juice') An acidic liquid obtained from sour grapes and other unripe fruit; it can be used in place of wine vinegar, and under the name *ābghooreh* is a common ingredient in Iranian cuisine.

Timeline

622	The *hejira* or *hijra* – the migration of the Prophet Muhammad and his followers from Mecca to Yathrib (Medina) – and the founding there of the first Muslim state
632–661	Period of the Rashidun ('rightly guided') caliphs, the first four successors to Muhammad (Abu Bakr al-Siddiq, Umar ibn al-Khattab, Uthman ibn Affan and Ali ibn Abi Talib), and the rapid expansion of the Islamic empire
661–750	Reign of the Umayyad dynasty with its capital at Damascus
680	Death of Muhammad's grandson Husayn ibn Ali at the Battle of Karbala in Iraq against the Umayyads signals an irrevocable split between Shia and Sunni Islam
750–1258	Reign of the Abbasid dynasty with its capital at Baghdad
756–1031	The Umayyad Emirate controls the Iberian Peninsula (al-Andalus), with its capital at Córdoba
909–1171	The Fatimids rule over North Africa, Sicily and Egypt; by 1000, they are the dominant Islamic power
1056–1147	The Berber Almoravid Emirate rules over North Africa and al-Andalus
1130–1269	The Almohad dynasty establishes its dominance over North Africa and (from 1160 on) Muslim Spain
1169–1260	Reign of the Kurdish Ayyubid dynasty, established by Salah ad-Din (Saladin), over Syria, Palestine and Egypt
1206–1526	The Sultanate of Delhi in Northern India
1230–1492	The Nasrids, reigning over a much-reduced emirate with its capital at Granada, are the last Arab Muslim dynasty to rule al-Andalus as the Christian Reconquista of Spain gains ground
1250–1517	The Mamelukes (formerly slave soldiers of the Ayubbids) establish Muslim dynasties throughout the Middle East until they are overthrown by the Ottoman Turks; They continue to rule in Egypt with Ottoman blessing until 1811

1300–1924	The Ottomans rule North Africa, the Fertile Crescent, Asia Minor and the Balkans; the empire is dismantled after the First World War
1501–1736	The Safavid dynasty reigns over Persia (Iran), with the capital at Isfahan
1526–1858	The Mughals overthrow the Delhi Sultanate and rule India (with capitals at Delhi and Lahore) until the founding of the British Raj
1798	The invasion of Egypt by Napoleon Bonaparte marks the beginning of modern European colonial intervention in the Middle East
1945–1955	Decolonisation of the Muslim states of the Middle East

Bibliography

Abala, Ken, *Food in Early Modern Europe*, Connecticut 2003.

Abaza, Mona, *The Changing Consumer Cultures of Egypt. Cairo's Urban Reshaping*, Cairo 2006.

Abaza, Mona, *The Cotton Plantation Remembered. An Egyptian Family Story*, Cairo 2013.

Achaya, Konganda T., *Indian Food. A Historical Companion*, Delhi 1994.

Bentzin, Anke, *Von der ersten in die zweite Heimat. Usbekische Migranten in Istanbul zwischen türkischer, türkistanischer und usbekischer Identität*, Würzburg 2013.

Basan, Ghillie, *Classic Turkish Cooking*, London 1997.

Basan, Ghillie, *The Middle Eastern Kitchen*. London 2001.

Bickel, Walter, *Nationalgerichte aus aller Welt*, Gießen (undated).

Bolens, Lucie, *La cuisine andalouse, un art de vivre*, Paris 1990.

Bolens, Lucie, *L' Andalousie du quotidien au sacré*, London 1991.

Braun, Mathilde, *Die Führung der bürgerlichen und feinen Küche*, 15th edn., Lingen 1951.

Brothwell, Don R. and Patricia Brothwell, *Food in Antiquity: A Survey of the Diet of Early Peoples*, Baltimore 1997.

Chévre, Mathilde, *Délices d'Orient*. Paris 2000.

Choueiri, Ramzi, *The Arabian Cookbook: Traditional Arab Cuisine with a Modern Twist*, New York 2012.

David, Elizabeth, *A Book of Mediterranean Food*, London 1950.

Dawson, Thomas: *The Good's Housewife's Jewel* (1596), with an introduction by Maggie Black: Southover Historic Cookery and Housekeeping Series, Sheffield 2002.

Degner, Rotraud, *Das Kochbuch fürs Leben*, Stuttgart 1957.

Dusy, Tanja and Ronald Schenkel, *Indien. Küche und Kultur*, Munich 2005.

Ehlert, Trude, *Das Kochbuch des Mittelalters. Rezepte aus alter Zeit*, Zurich 1990.

Faroqhi, Suraiya, *Subjects of the Sultan: Culture and Daily Life in the Ottoman Empire*, London 2000.

Fischer, Johan, *The Halal Frontier. Muslim Consumers in a Globalized Market*, Basingstoke 2011.

Flandrin, Jean-Louis and Massimo Montanari (eds.), *Food. A Culinary History*, New York 1999.

Fragner, Bert G., 'From the Caucasus to the Roof of the World: A Culinary Adventure', Sami Zubaida and Richard Tapper (eds.), *Culinary Cultures of the Middle East*, London 1994, pp. 49–62.

Fragner, Bert G., 'Social Reality and Culinary Fiction: The Perspective of Cookbooks from Iran and Central Asia', Sami Zubaida and Richard Tapper (eds.), *Culinary Cultures of the Middle East*, London 1994, pp. 63–71.

Frembgen, Jürgen W. (ed.), *Derwische und Zuckerbäcker. Bilder aus einem orientalischen Basar*, Munich 1996.

Friedlander, Michael and Cilly Kugelmann (eds.), *Koscher und Co. Über Essen und Religion*, Berlin 2009.

Gelder, Geert Jan van, *Of Dishes and Discourse. Classical Arabic Literary Representations of Food*, Richmond 2000.

El Glaoui, Mina, *Ma Cuisine Marocaine*, Paris 1987.

Goodwin, Godfrey, *The Janissaries*, London 1994.

Goody, Jack, *Cooking, Cuisine and Class. A Study in Comparative Sociology*, Cambridge 1982.

Goody, Jack, *Food and Love. A Cultural History of East and West*, London 1998.

Gruschke, Andreas, Andreas Schörner and Astrid Zimmermann, *Tee. Süßer Tau des Himmels*, Munich 2001.

Guinaudeau, Zette, *Fès vu par sa cuisine. Gastronomie marocaine*, 9th edn., Saint Cloud 1976.

Guinaudeau-Franc, Zette, *Les secrets des cuisines en terre marocaine*, Paris 1981.

Hage, Salma, *The Lebanese Kitchen*, London 2012.

Halıcı, Nevin, *Nevin Halıcı's Turkish Cookbook*, London 1989.

Halıcı, Nevin, *Sufi Cuisine*, London 2005.

Harms, Florian and Lutz Jäkel, *Kulinarisches Arabien*, Vienna 2004.

Harris, Marvin, *Cows, Pigs, Wars and Witches, The Riddles of Culture*, New York 1977.

al Hashimi, Miriam, *Traditional Arabic Cooking*, Reading 1993.

Hattox, Ralph S., *Coffee and Coffeehouses. The Origins of a Social Beverage in the Medieval Near East*, Seattle 1985.

Heine, Peter, *Weinstudien. Untersuchungen zu Anbau, Produktion und Konsum des Weins im arabisch-islamischen Mittelalter*, Wiesbaden 1982.

Heine, Peter, *Kulinarische Studien. Untersuchungen zur Kochkunst im arabisch-islamischen Mittelalter*, Wiesbaden 1988.

Heine, Peter, *Food Culture in the Near East, Middle East, and North Africa*, Westport, Connecticut 2004.

Heise, Ulla and Beatrix Freifrau von Wolff Metternich (eds.), *Coffeum wirft die Jungfrau um. Kaffee und Erotik in Porzellan und Grafik aus drei Jahrhunderten*, Leipzig 1998.

Holzen, Heinz von, Lother Arsana and Wendy Hutton, *The Food of Indonesia: Authentic Recipes from the Spice Islands*, Singapore 1995.

Hundsbichler, Helmut (ed.), *Kommunikation zwischen Orient und Okzident. Alltag und Sachkultur*, Vienna 1994.

Husain, Salma, *Nuskha-e-Shahjahani. Pulaos from the Royal Kitchen of Shah Jahan*, New Delhi 2004.

İlkin, Nur and Sheilah Kaufman, *The Turkish Cookbook. Regional Recipes and Stories*, London 2012.

Jäkel, Lutz, *Dubai – New Arabian Cuisine*, London 2007.

Jaouhari, Alain, *Maroc – La Cuisine de ma Mère*. Paris 2002.

Kitchen, Leanne, *Turkey – Recipes and Tales from the Road*. London 2011.

Küster, Hansjörg, *Am Anfang war das Korn. Eine andere Geschichte der Menschheit*, Munich 2013.

Lewicka, Paulina B., *Food and Foodways of Medieval Cairenes. Aspects of Life in an Islamic Metropolis of the Eastern Mediterranean*, Leiden 2011.

Leyel, Hilda and Olga Hartley, *The Gentle Art of Cookery*, London 2013 (1st edn. 1925).

Lovatt-Smith, Lisa, *Moroccan Interiors*, Munich 1995.

Lutz-Auras, Ludmilla and Pierre Gottschlich (eds.), *Aus dem politischen Küchenkabinett. Eine kurze Kulturgeschichte der Kulinarik*, Baden-Baden 2013.

Mählis, Madlen, 'Eating gingzhen in China'. Master's thesis at the London School of Oriental and African Studies. Unpublished manuscript 2011.

Marín, Manuela and David Waines (eds.), *Kanz al-fawa'id fi tanwi'al-mawa'id* (Medieval Arab/Islamic Culinary Art), Beirut 1993.

Marín, Manuela and David Waines (eds.), *La Alimentación en las culturas islámicas. Una collección de estudios*, Madrid 1994.

Marín, Manuela and Cristina de la Puente (eds.), *El banquete de las Palabras: La alimentación en los textos árabes*, Madrid 2005.

Martino da Como, *The Art of Cooking*. English translation by Jeremy Parzen, Berkeley 2005.

al-Mausili, Zubaida, et al., *Min fann al-tabkh al-saʿudi*, 4th edn., Jeddah 1990.

Mintz, Sidney W., *Sweetness and Power. The Place of Sugar in Modern History*, New York 1985.

Morse, Kitty, *Cooking at the Kasbah. Recipes from My Moroccan Kitchen*, San Francisco 1998.

Moryoussef, Viviane et Nina, *La cuisine juive marocaine*, Paris 1983.

Müller, Christa, *Wurzeln schlagen in der Fremde. Die internationalen Gärten und ihre Bedeutung für Integrationsprozesse*, Munich 2002.

Nasrallah, Nawal, *Delights from the Garden of Eden. A Cookbook and a History of the Iraqi Cuisine*, Bloomington 2003.

Ottolenghi, Yotam and Sami Tamimi, *Ottolenghi: The Cookbook*, London 2008.

Ottolenghi, Yotam and Sami Tamimi, *Jerusalem: A Cookbook*, London 2012.

Peschke, Hans-Peter von/Werner Feldmann, *Das Kochbuch der Renaissance*, Düsseldorf 1997.

Peter, Peter, *Kulturgeschichte der italienischen Küche*, 2nd edn., Munich 2007.

Platina, Bartolomeo, *Platina, on Right Pleasure and Good Health. A Critical Edition and Translation of De honesta voluptate et valetudine by Mary Ella Milham*, Tempe 1998.

Reimers, Britta (ed.), *Gärten und Politik. Vom Kultivieren der Erde*, Munich 2010.

Roden, Claudia, *A Book of Middle Eastern Food*, London 1968.

Roden, Claudia, *Mediterranean Cookery*, London 1987.

Roden, Claudia, *Tamarind & Saffron. Favourite Recipes from the Middle East*, London 1999.

Rowe, Silvena, *Purple Citrus & Sweet Perfume. Cuisine of the Eastern Mediterranean*, London 2010.

Roy, Olivier, *Globalised Islam. The Search for a New Ummah*, London 2004.

Sauner-Nebioglu, Marie-Hélène, *Evolution des pratiques alimentaires en Turquie: Analyse comparative*, Berlin 1995.

Schievelbusch, Wolfgang, *Das Paradies, der Geschmack und die Vernunft. Eine Geschichte der Genußmittel*, Munich 1980.

Seidel-Pielen, Eberhard, *Aufgespießt. Wie der Döner über die Deutschen kam*, Hamburg 1996.

Serjeant, Robert B. and Ronald Lewcock (eds.), *Sana'a, an Arabian Islamic City*, London 1983.

Taneja, Meera, *Pakistani Cookery*, London 1985.

Tariq, Zubeida, *From Zubeida Tariq's Kitchen*, Lahore 2005.

Teuteberg, Hans Jürgen, Gerhard Neumann and Alois Wierlacher (eds.), *Essen und kulturelle Identität. Europäische Perspektiven*, Berlin 1997.

Titley, Norah M. (ed. and transl.), *The Ni'matnama Manuscript of the Sultans of Mandu*, London 2005.

Trummer, Manuel, *Pizza, Döner, McKropolis. Entwicklungen, Erscheinungsformen und Wertewandel internationaler Gastronomie, am Beispiel der Stadt Regensburg*, Münster 2009.

al-Tujibi, Ibn Razin, *Fadalat al-khiwan fi tayyibat al-ta'am wa l-alwan*, ed. Muhammad Benchekroun, Rabat 1981.

Vámbéry, Ármin (Hermann), *Sittenbilder aus dem Morgenlande*, Berlin 1876.

Waines, David, *In a Caliph's Kitchen. Mediaeval Arabic Cooking for the Modern Gourmet*, London 1989.

al-Warraq, Ibn Sayyar, *Annals of the Caliph's Kitchens*. English Translation by Nawal Nasrallah, Leiden 2007.

Watson, Andrew M., *Agricultural Innovation in the Early Islamic World. The Diffusion of Crops and Farming Techniques, 700–1100*, Cambridge 1983.

Westrip, Joyce, *Moghul Cooking. India's Courtly Cuisine*, London 1997.

Wierlacher, Alois (ed.), *Gastlichkeit. Rahmenthema der Kulinaristik*, Berlin 2011.

Wilkins, John, David Harvey and Mike Dobson (eds.), *Food in Antiquity*, Exeter 1995.

Wolfsgruber, Linda, *Pistazien und Rosenduft. Die Kunst der persischen Küche*, Vienna 2007.

Zeller, Benjamin E., Marie W. Dallam, Reid L. Neilson and Nora L. Rubel (eds.), *Religion, Food, and Eating in North America*, New York 2014.

Peter Heine, who was born in 1944, taught at the universities of Münster and Bonn and was until his retirement in 2009 Professor of Islamic Studies at the Humboldt University in Berlin. He is the author of a number of books on such diverse topics as the place of women within Islam, Islamophobia in the West, the origins of modern Islamic fundamentalism, and the history of food and wine in Arab societies of the Middle Ages.

Peter Lewis read Modern Languages at St. Edmund Hall, Oxford and Albert -Ludwigs-Universität, Freiburg, graduating in 1981. After careers in university teaching and publishing, he now works as a freelance translator and author. His recent translations include Asfa-Wossen Asserate's *King of Kings. The Triumph and Tragedy of Emperor Haile Selassie I of Ethiopia* (Haus Publishing, 2015), Johannes Fried's *Charlemagne. A Biography* (Harvard University Press, 2016), Dierk Walter's *Colonial Violence* (Hurst Publishers, 2017), and Gunnar Decker's *Hesse: The Wanderer and His Shadow* (Harvard University Press, 2018).